Advancing Nonprofit Stewardship
Through Self-Regulation

Advancing Nonprofit Stewardship Through Self-Regulation: Translating Principles into Practice

Christopher Corbett

Kumarian Press
An Imprint of Stylus Publishing

Advancing Nonprofit Stewardship Through Self-Regulation:
Translating Principles into Practice
Published in 2011 in the United States of America by Kumarian Press,
22883 Quicksilver Drive, Sterling, VA 20166 USA.

Design by Pro Production Graphic Services
Copyedit by Bob Land
Proofread by Beth Richards
Index by Robert Swanson
The text of this book is set in 10.5/13 Adobe Garamond

Printed in the USA on acid-free paper by Thomson-Shore.

∞ The paper used in this publication meets the minimum requirements of the American National Standard for Information Sciences—Permanence of Paper for Printed
Library Materials, ANSI Z39.48–1984

Library of Congress Cataloging-in-Publication Data

Corbett, Christopher, 1951–
Advancing nonprofit stewardship through self-regulation : translating
    principles into practice / Christopher Corbett.
        p.   cm.
    Includes bibliographical references and index.
    ISBN 978-1-56549-408-4 (pbk. : alk. paper) — ISBN 978-1-56549-410-7
        (library ebook) — ISBN 978-1-56549-411-4 (consumer ebook)
    1. Nonprofit organizations—United States—Moral and ethical aspects.
2. Nonprofit organizations—United States—Finance. 3. Nonprofit
organizations—United States. I. Title.
    HD2769.2.U6C67 2011
    658'.048—dc22
                                                    2011001863

To my father,
James F. Corbett
1919–2009

Contents

**Part 1 Thirty-three Principles for Good Governance
and Ethical Practice from the Panel on the Nonprofit
Sector Convened by Independent Sector**

Part 2 Putting Principles into Action

Foreword

In spite of its small size, this book is very important and potentially useful for all nonprofit organization and association CEOs, other top managers, board members/trustees, officers, and other leaders. In my view, based on nearly half a century of research and leadership experience in the Voluntary Nonprofit Sector (VNPS), no responsible leader or manager of a nonprofit organization or association in the United States should endanger his or her group by failing to read this book carefully and applying its suggestions to his or her nonprofit. Because it addresses near-universal governance principles, the book also applies to the situation of nonprofit organizations (or nongovernmental organizations—NGOs, as they are often called) in many other nations. Of course, specific laws and regulations affecting nonprofit organizations vary greatly across the nations of the world.

A new age of nonprofit organization/association accountability has begun recently in America. This age is also dawning elsewhere, especially in the developed nations of the world. A few large, mainstream (widely respected) U.S. nonprofit organizations have engaged in or been involved in various kinds of high-profile misconduct and deviance, especially in the past two decades. The mass media coverage of these few major scandals has prompted increasing criticism of all nonprofit organizations and associations, of whatever size, by both the general public and government leaders, as well as VNPS leaders.

Some critics of the VNPS among business sector leaders and legal experts see the whole structure of special privileges for nonprofit groups to be "unfair." Such critics often feel strongly that nonprofit organizations, especially those that compete with businesses, have an unfair advantage over for-profit businesses. The crux of this unfair-competition argument is usually that the tax exemptions granted to nonprofit organizations are often undeserved, because the organizations are doing the same, or same kind of, service work as for-profit businesses that must pay taxes. (See, for instance, Bennett and Di Lorenzo's *Unfair Competition: The Profits of Nonprofits* [1989]; Brody's *Agents Without Principals: The Economic Convergence of the Nonprofit and For-Profit Organizational Forms* [1996]; Gaul and Borowski's *Free Ride: The Tax-Exempt Economy* [1993].)

Weisbrod's edited volume *To Profit or Not to Profit* (1998), with contributions from several economists and other social scientists, lends support to this argument. As a whole, that book shows that many nonprofit organizations are becoming more and more like private businesses—shifting away from dependence on private charitable donations toward commercial sales activities and user fees for services. This trend could eventually lead to a very basic challenge to the whole structure of tax exemption in America for the larger nonprofit organizations. However, most nonprofit groups in America in terms of sheer numbers (not assets or income) are small, local membership associations, as D. Smith has shown in his book *Grassroots Associations* (2000, chap. 2). Such small, often all-volunteer groups still depend mainly on dues and donations for income.

A second major criticism of the VNPS comes from those who point to the substantial—sometimes nearly total—dependence of many social service nonprofit organizations on government funds. Researchers have shown that social service nonprofit organizations have, in the last several decades, become increasingly dependent on government agency contracts and funding for their work, in the United States as well as in other modern welfare states (see Gidron et al., *Government and the Third Sector* [1992]; Kramer et al., *Privatization in Four European Countries* [1993]; Rekart, *Public Funds, Private Provision* [1993]; and S. Smith and Lipsky, *Nonprofits for Hire* [1993]).

One source cited in Wagner (2000, 131) estimated that about 61% of government funding of social services in America comes through the VNPS. With these contracts from government agencies come various kinds of requirements and essentially certain forms of government control of nonprofit organizations. Proponents of the independence of the VNPS find these developments very troubling.

A third major set of outspoken VNPS critics point to scandals, corruption, and the "dark side" (especially deviance and misconduct, but also dysfunctions) of the VNPS. Some of these critics give special attention to fundamentally deviant groups that pervasively and from the start flout laws and basic moral principles in some basic way. Others criticize more mainstream nonprofit organizations for lapses in accountability and regulation—whether government regulation or self-regulation.

From my perspective, this dark side of the VNPS manifests in three broad types across a spectrum from extreme degrees of deviance/misconduct/harm to moderate to mild degrees. For a full discussion of the whole range of VNPS deviance in and by nonprofit groups and its underlying causes, see my book *Deviations: The Dark Side of Goodness in the Angelic Nonprofit Sector* (forthcoming).

    1. **Extreme** degrees of deviance and misconduct in the American VNPS are apparent in three main types of nonprofit groups: political, religious, and emotional expression.

    a. A few examples of books dealing with extreme deviance in American nonprofit *political* groups are Emerson's *American Jihad: The Terrorists Living Among Us* (2002), George and Wilcox's *American Extremists* (1996), and Tilly's *Social Movements, 1768–2004* (2004).

    b. Some examples of books focused on extreme American nonprofit *religious* groups would be Bromley and Melton's *Cults, Religion, and Violence* (2004), Lewis and Petersen's *Controversial New Religions* (2005), and Snow's *Deadly Cults* (2003).

    c. Three examples of books focused on extreme American nonprofit *emotional expression* groups of the sensual/erotic expression variety would be Constantine and Constantine's *Group Marriage* (1973), Gould's *The Lifestyle: A Look at the Erotic Rites of Swingers* (2000), and Sagarin's *Structure and Ideology in an Association of Deviants* (1975). Two other examples of books focused on extreme American nonprofit emotional expression groups, but of the hatred/anger expression variety, would be Lavigne's *Hell's Angels* (1997) and Sims' *The Klan* (1996).

    2. More **moderate** degrees of deviance and misconduct in the American VNPS are described in books on various social movement organizations, such as Ford's *Iron-Jawed Angels: The Suffrage Militancy of the National Woman's Party* (1991), Jasper and Nelkin's *The Animal Rights Crusade* (1992), Lee's *Earth First! Environment Apocalypse* (1995), and Levitas's *The Terrorist Next Door: The Militia Movement and the Radical Right* (2002).

3. Incidents of comparatively **mild** degrees of deviance and misconduct in the American VNPS occur in mainstream, highly respectable nonprofit organizations where the deviance tends to be more isolated to particular individuals or brief time periods, rather than representing a major goal of the whole organization. Books describing these cases include Boyle's *Scout's Honor: Sexual Abuse in America's Most Trusted Institution* (1994), Fishman's *The Faithless Fiduciary and the Quest for Charitable Accountability, 1200–2005* (2007), and Fortune and Longwood's *Sexual Abuse in the Catholic Church: Trusting the Clergy?* (2003).

One of the most striking and highly publicized examples of nonprofit organization misconduct since 1990 in America was the William Aramony scandal at the United Way of America, as John Glaser described in *The United Way Scandal: An Insider's Account of What Went Wrong and Why* (1994). While Aramony was president of the United Way of America, he engaged in criminal misuse of his organization's funds, among other misconduct. He was arrested, tried, found guilty of various crimes, and then served time in prison. United Way donations for the next few years fell off significantly, costing the United Way movement nationally (including the United Way of America umbrella organization) hundreds of millions of dollars.

This widely publicized scandal was notable because it occurred in a high-prestige and very well-known American charity—a sacred cow that previously had been rarely criticized, let alone scrutinized (but see D. Smith's much earlier critique [1978]). This specific scandal opened the door to more critical evaluation of other major charities and nonprofit organizations in America that had before been immune to reproach. Most VNPS leaders and the general public also generally ignored the earlier "new religious movement" or cult scandals of the late 1970s (e.g., the Peoples Temple and Jonestown Massacre in 1978; see Weightman 1983) and in the 1980s–1990s (e.g., the Children of God; see Van Zandt 1991). Such horrific events as the mass-murder-suicide in Jonestown and the deviant sexual activities of the Jesus people cult were usually dismissed as the bizarre acts of cult freaks having nothing to do with the mainstream of the VNPS and its leading nonprofit organizations.

But when the United Way of America was involved in a major scandal in the early 1990s, the reaction was very different. This single, painful event gravely challenged American society's longstanding presumption of goodness in the whole VNPS, considered the Angelic Sector (see D. Smith et al., *A Dictionary of Nonprofit Terms and Concepts* [2006, 21], for a discussion of the origins of this term). Several subsequent high-profile scandals among large, mainstream nonprofit organizations in America have stoked the fires of VNPS critics.

Wagner (2000) wrote a major critique of the American VNPS (see chap. 5 of *What's Love Got to Do with It? A Critical Look at American Charity*, titled "The Sanctified Sector: The 'Nonprofit'"). Specialists in the study of the VNPS have paid relatively little attention to the dark side until very recently, according to academic conference papers by D. Smith (2008a, 2008b). Only a handful of academic journal articles have taken a broad look at deviance and misconduct in mainstream nonprofit organizations (Gibelman and Gelman 2001, 2004; Greenlee et al. 2007), all of them in the past decade.

The problems of misconduct and deviance have been growing sufficiently important on the radar screens of nonprofit organization managers and board members that Zack (2003) has written a book for such leaders; see *Fraud and Abuse in Nonprofit Organizations: A Guide to Prevention and Detection*.

Interest in the accountability in and of nonprofit organizations has increased rapidly in the past decade or two (see Cutt and Murray, *Accountability and Effectiveness Evaluation in Nonprofit Organizations* [2000]; Fishman, *The Faithless Fiduciary and the Quest for Charitable Accountability, 1200–2005* [2007]), and not just in America (see Jordan and van Tuijl, *NGO Accountability* [2007]). The nonprofit management journal *The Nonprofit Quarterly* published as a special issue (vol. 12, 2005) an excellent overview of the recent situation, with the title *Regulation and Accountability: The New Wave*.

The foregoing review of the situation and accompanying literature is the larger context in which Corbett's present book must be seen and understood. Deviance and misconduct in and by American nonprofit organizations has led specifically to growing congressional consideration of greater federal government oversight of U.S. nonprofit organizations.

The two provisions of the Sarbanes-Oxley Act of 2002 that apply to nonprofit organizations (as well as to businesses) are concrete examples of tightening U.S. government regulation of American nonprofits. This legislation is already in place as a general result of the VNPS behaviors briefly sketched above. Certain powerful U.S. legislators have informally threatened stronger and more extensive government regulation if the VNPS does not engage in far better self-regulation going forward.

The mainstream VNPS coalition and infrastructure organization called Independent Sector (see O'Connell, *Powered by Coalition* [1997]) has taken the lead in fostering better governance in American nonprofit organizations of all sizes, with the prompting of the U.S. Senate Finance Committee. Under president and CEO Diana Aviv, Independent Sector convened a panel on the nonprofit sector in October 2004. This panel was intended to be "an independent group of nonprofit leaders who will recommend actions to strengthen the governance, ethical conduct, and accountability of charitable organizations." (See its website www.independentsector.org/panel/main.htm.)

In October 2007 the panel released both a full-length and an abridged version of its final report, *Principles for Good Governance and Ethical Practice: A Guide for Charities and Foundations* (available at www.independent sector.org). The report presents 33 principles for good governance, organized under four main categories: Legal Compliance and Public Disclosure, Effective Governance, Strong Financial Oversight, and Responsible Fundraising.

■ ESSENTIAL CONTRIBUTIONS OF THE PRESENT BOOK

Christopher Corbett takes the principles of the panel's report down to the nitty-gritty, practical level of individual nonprofit organization leadership. He translates all 33 of the Principles of Self-Regulation into practice by devising and presenting by-laws for these principles. Corbett relied in part on the responses to a survey of A-rated nonprofits' by-laws (65 organizations sent their by-laws for Corbett's analysis).

This book makes it very easy for any nonprofit organization or association that is formally organized to have its board of directors (or trustees) consider specific implementation of by-law changes to address any or all of the 33 good-governance principles.

The content of this book reflects the author's atypical and distinctively useful combination of experiences and perspectives. First, Corbett has been a nonprofit researcher and longtime member of and participant in the Association for Research on Nonprofit Organizations and Voluntary Action (ARNOVA; see www.arnova.org). ARNOVA is the first, oldest (founded in 1971), largest, and most prestigious of the world's many interdisciplinary professional associations for doing, disseminating, or using research on the VNPS. Additionally, Corbett has been, since its formation in 1992, a member of the International Society for Third Sector Research (ISTR; see www.istr.org). ISTR boasts of researchers from more than 80 nations; ARNOVA has representatives from just over 30 countries.

Second, Corbett has been community psychologist (M.A., Sage Graduate School) since 1994, with membership in Division 27 of the American Psychological Association. This division constitutes the Society for Community Research and Action (SCRA), which promotes systemic interventions at the highest levels possible to improve society using psychological principles and research results with a focus on prevention.

Third, and not least important for the validity of this book's practical ideas, Corbett was a state government regulator for more than 30 years. He is passionate about applying the totality of his career and life experiences to help nonprofit organization boards and other leaders implement system-level change at the highest levels. This book has a strong potential for preventing future deviance and misconduct in all kinds and sizes of nonprofit organizations, not only in the United States but also in many other nations of the world.

This book should be required reading for anyone interested in practical steps that nonprofits can take to help ensure that their board members have not merely the responsibility to govern but also the actual authority to perform their oversight functions. The book is a practical manual and a blueprint for how to implement the 33 Principles for Good Governance and Ethical Practice. Various by-laws empower board members to obtain the necessary information and guarantee the opportunity for board member participation at crucial junctures in the governance function.

Used properly and fully, the information in this book can empower boards to take governance control more assertively during difficult times. Wise nonprofit boards that do so can help greatly in preventing the deviance, misconduct, abuse, fraud, and public scandals that have become so common in recent decades. Each scandal, regardless of its size or scope, damages and embarrasses the VNPS and its organizations. Scandals seriously undermine public as well as policymaker confidence in the integrity of nonprofit organizations.

I believe that retention of some form of tax-exempt status is imperative for the American VNPS to survive. In the long run a substantial degree of freedom and independence from government is also necessary. Nazi Party leader Adolf Hitler took official power in January 1933, appointed chancellor and dictator of Germany by the elected president Hindenburg. One of Hitler's top priorities was to stifle and eliminate all possible collective/organized opposition that might arise from the German VNPS. Hitler thus almost immediately initiated a thorough program of VNPS takeover, as William Allen describes in detail from the perspective of one particular small town (see *The Nazi Seizure of Power* [1984]). This dictatorial government either took operational control of cooperative/submissive nonprofit organizations and associations, or eliminated (killed or caused to disband) the noncooperative/resistant associations and other nonprofits.

Hitler accomplished his goal of total government control of the German VNPS in about 18 months. But a stealth version of such VNPS control in a country can also take place piecemeal over many years. The United States is not immune to such a process, especially in this era of a "war on terror." We emphatically do not have a dictator in our nation at present, in my view (January 2011). But well-meaning federal or state legislators could easily bring ever more heavy-handed government regulation down on the VNPS in America if the vast majority of our nonprofits are not successful at self-regulation, along the lines of the 33 Principles.

We need to pursue clearly improved and quickly implemented self-regulation of nonprofit organizations in America if we hope to maintain our eroding freedom of association in an age of terrorism. The practices and methods of implementation presented in this book reflect a level of insight that is unusually thoughtful while being respectful of board members' rights to choose between more aggressive or less aggressive alternatives.

Thus, Corbett's book provides nonprofit board members/trustees with specific by-law solutions but often enables them to readily modify or adjust the exact implementation, consistent with the board's needs and prerogatives, and the organizational mission. This book could be considered as presenting a board empowerment model of nonprofit governance. It promotes and enables board members' participation in the governance process, allowing them to perform their duties and responsibilities more effectively.

Corbett's book is useful for all board members and nonprofit managers concerned about nonprofit governance and accountability today. But it is also a helpful reference when a specific issue or controversy arises, providing possible solutions that a board can implement immediately, based upon the motion of a single board member. The book empowers board members to put a stake into the ground on many difficult and controversial issues by developing proposed by-law solutions that a board can use for discussion purposes, to build consensus on, and to ultimately spur a board level vote on one or more possible resolutions.

This book may well act as a catalyst in producing conflict in an effort to solve difficult problems, but conflict often produces compromises and mutual adjustments, yielding solutions achievable in no other way. More-over, because of the near universality of the relevance of the principles, the book is potentially useful to international nongovernment organizations (INGOs) that struggle with many of the same governance dilemmas as U.S.-based nonprofits.

Nonprofit researchers can use this book to glean new insights into prac-tical applications of good governance principles and shape the way in which they conduct their research to increase its usefulness and applicability to benefit nonprofit organization boards, and to the VNPS indirectly.

Corbett strongly recommends that all nonprofit boards implement by-laws relating to the principles of good governance and ethical practice. I strongly agree with him. Researchers developing alternative approaches and paradigms should be as strongly encouraged and welcomed in order to pro-vide nonprofits additional choices. The stakes are high, as is the need, for more useful, informed guidance for nonprofit boards.

From a deep concern over the consequences of nonprofit scandals on the VNPS and public alike, the author has developed many practical rec-ommendations on how to prevent such negative outcomes. In that process, Corbett has created a highly useful implementation guide and reference book that belongs on the desk of all board members, officers, and managers of nonprofit organizations who truly care about nonprofit governance, ac-countability, effectiveness, and organizational survival.

In conclusion, this outstanding book, as a practical manual for nonprofit organization leaders, puts the ball of ethical nonprofit governance and ac-countability squarely in the board members' court—*precisely* where it needs to be if real change is to occur. Significant progress in improving the gover-nance and self-regulation of formal nonprofits is well within our reach. But achieving such better governance depends on whether most board members and managers of nonprofit organizations actually seize that opportunity *now.*

—*David Horton Smith, PhD*
Professor Emeritus of Sociology and
Research Professor of Sociology, Boston College.
Visiting Professor of Nonprofit Research,
City University, London, UK.

Founder of the Association for Research on Nonprofit
Organizations and Voluntary Action (ARNOVA) and the
Nonprofit and Voluntary Sector Quarterly (*NVSQ*) journal.
(www.davidhortonsmith.net)

■ REFERENCES

Allen, W.S. 1984. *The Nazi seizure of power.* New York: Franklin Watts.

Bennett, J.T., and T.J. Di Lorenzo. 1989. *Unfair competition: The profits of non-profits.* New York: Hamilton.

Boyle, Patrick. 1994. *Scout's honor.* Rocklin, CA: Prima Publishing.

Brody, E. 1996. Agents without principals: The economic convergence of the nonprofit and for-profit organizational forms. *New York Law School Law Review* 40:457–536.

Bromley, David G., and J. Gordon Melton. 2004. *Cults, religion, and violence.* New York: Cambridge University Press.

Constantine, Larry L., and Joan M. Constantine. 1973. *Group marriage.* New York: Collier MacMillan.

Cutt, J., and V. Murray. 2000. *Accountability and effectiveness evaluation in non-profit organizations.* London: Routledge.

Emerson, Steven. 2002. *American jihad: The terrorists living among us.* New York: Free Press.

Fishman, James J. 2007. *The faithless fiduciary and the quest for charitable accountability 1200–2005.* Durham, NC: Carolina Academic Press.

Ford, Linda G. 1991. *Iron-jawed angels: The suffrage militancy of the national woman's party 1912–1920.* Lanham, MD: University Press of America.

Fortune, Marie M., and W. Merle Longwood. 2003. *Sexual abuse in the Catholic Church: Trusting the clergy?* Binghamton, NY: Haworth Pastoral Press.

Gaul, G.M., and N.A. Borowski. 1993. *Free ride: The tax-exempt economy.* Kansas City, MO: Andrews and McMeel.

George, John, and Laird Wilcox. 1996. *American extremists.* Amherst, NY: Prometheus Books.

Gibelman, Margaret, and Sheldon R. Gelman. 2001. Very public scandals: Nongovernmental organizations in trouble. *Voluntas* 12, no. 1:49–66.

———. 2004. A loss of credibility: Patterns of wrongdoing among nonprofit organizations. *Voluntas* 15, no. 4:355–81.

Gidron, B., R. Kramer, and L. Salamon. 1992. *Government and the third sector.* San Francisco: Jossey-Bass.

Glaser, J.S. 1994. *The United Way scandal: An insider's account of what went wrong and why.* New York: John Wiley.

Greenlee, J., M. Fisher, T. Gordon, and E. Keating. 2007. An investigation of fraud in nonprofit organizations: Occurrences and deterrents. *Nonprofit and Voluntary Sector Quarterly* 36, no. 4:676–94.

Gould, Terry. 2000. *The lifestyle.* Buffalo, NY: Firefly Books.

Jasper, James M., and Dorothy Nelkin. 1992. *The animal rights crusade: The growth of a moral protest.* New York: Free Press.

Jordan, Lisa, and Peter van Tuijl, eds. 2007. *NGO accountability: Politics, principles and innovations.* London: Earthscan.

Kramer, R.M., H. Lorentzen, W. Melief, and S. Pasquinelli. 1993. *Privatization in four European countries.* Armonk, NY: M.E. Sharpe.

Lavigne, Yves. 1993. *Hell's angels.* New York: Carol Publishing Group.

Lee, Martha F. 1995. *Earth first: Environmental apocalypse.* Syracuse, NY: Syracuse University Press.

Levitas, Daniel. 2002. *The terrorist next door: The militia movement and the radical right.* New York: Thomas Dunne Books/St. Martin's Press.

Lewis, J.R., and Jesper Petersen, eds. 2005. *Controversial new religions.* Oxford: Oxford University Press.

O'Connell, B. 1997. *Powered by coalition: The story of Independent Sector.* San Francisco: Jossey-Bass.

Rekart, J. 1993. *Public funds, private provision: The role of the voluntary sector.* Vancouver, Canada: UBC Press.

Sagarin, Edward. 1975. *Structure and ideology in an association of deviants.* New York: Arno Press.

Sims, Patsy. 1996. *The Klan.* 2nd ed. Lexington: University Press of Kentucky.

Smith, David Horton. 1978. The philanthropy business, *Society* 15:8–15.

———. 2000. *Grassroots associations.* Thousand Oaks, CA: Sage.

———. 2008a. Accepting and understanding the "dark side" of the nonprofit sector: One key part of building a healthier civil society. Paper presented at the ARNOVA Conference, November 2008, Philadelphia.

———. 2008b. Comparative study of fundamentally deviant nonprofit groups and their role in global civil society and democratic cultures as a new frontier for third sector research: Evidence for prevalence of the false "Angelic Nonprofit Groups Flat-Earth Paradigm." Paper presented at the Biennial Conference of the International Society for Third Sector Research, Barcelona, Spain, July 9–12, 2008.

———. Forthcoming. *Deviations: The dark side of goodness in the angelic nonprofit sector.* Unpublished book manuscript in progress.

———, R.A. Stebbins, and M.A. Dover. 2006. *A dictionary of nonprofit terms and concepts.* Bloomington: Indiana University Press.

Smith, S.R., and M. Lipsky. 1993. *Nonprofits for hire.* Cambridge, MA: Harvard University Press.

Snow, Robert L. 2003. *Deadly cults: The crimes of true believers.* Westport, CT: Praeger.

Tilly, Charles. 2004. *Social movements, 1768–2004.* Boulder, CO: Paradigm Publishers.

Van Zandt, D.E. 1991. *Living in the Children of God.* Princeton, NJ: Princeton University Press.

Wagner, D. 2000. *What's love got to do with it? A critical look at American charity.* New York: New Press.

Weightman, J.M. 1983. *Making sense of the Jonestown suicides.* Lewiston, NY: Edwin Mellen Press.

Weisbrod, B.A., ed. 1998. *To profit or not to profit: The commercial transformation of the nonprofit sector.* New York: Cambridge University Press.

Zack, G.M. 2003. *Fraud and abuse in nonprofit organizations.* Hoboken, NJ: Wiley.

Preface

My purpose and hope for this book are to help promote and improve the self-regulation of nonprofit and voluntary organizations.

Important progress in building consensus for improved self-regulation is already taking place. Contributing to this public policy trend was passage of the Sarbanes-Oxley Act of 2002. Subsequently, U.S. senators Chuck Grassley and Max Baucus requested Diana Aviv, president, Independent Sector (IS), to convene a panel that would recommend actions to strengthen ethics and nonprofit practice. From this panel, IS produced reports in June 2005 and April 2006. In February 2007 the IS Advisory Committee issued 31 Draft Principles. After considering the last round of comments, in October 2007 the panel issued a report recommending 33 Principles for nonprofits to adopt.

In this book I propose various strategies and practices to enable implementation of these principles. I urge that researchers and practitioners create competing strategies to provide nonprofits with a choice. Further, because many principles and practices promote accountability and transparency, which are universal values, I believe this book has relevance and application beyond the United States to NGOs and voluntary associations internationally.

Having spent more than 30 years in government in the regulation of public utilities, I have a keen awareness and appreciation for the strengths, limits, and costs of government regulation. Therefore, my fervent hope is that you will be able to assist in improving the self-regulation of nonprofit and voluntary associations—preserving their fragile resources and autonomy to limit or mitigate the need for further government regulation and intrusion, which would come at direct and substantial cost to all nonprofits and the communities they serve.

—C.J. Corbett

Acknowledgments

Several acknowledgments are in order for creating the conditions under which this book may help promote the improved self-regulation of the nonprofit sector.

First, I'd like to acknowledge our national leaders, Senator Max Baucus and Senator Chuck Grassley—for understanding the critical importance of industry consensus in promoting improved sector self-regulation—as well as Independent Sector, particularly Diana Aviv, for rising to the great challenges of actually helping to build that consensus.

Second, the Panel on the Nonprofit Sector must be recognized, along with the many parties who participated in the painstaking efforts required to develop the 33 Principles, as well as those who provided the substantial funding essential for this national effort.

Third, I want to recognize the hundreds of nonprofit organizations, including many foundations, that formally signed on to support the Panel's Report or the 33 Principles on Self-Regulation, or both. Their public commitment and support speak volumes as to their individual commitments to improved industry self-regulation by strengthening the governance, accountability, and transparency of the nonprofit sector.

Last but certainly not least, great appreciation is due to the nonprofit organizations that were willing to share their hard-earned governance wisdom by providing their by-laws, demonstrating how they had actually implemented and incorporated that wisdom within their formal governance structures.

Introduction

Government and nonprofit sector representatives have made significant progress in building consensus on the need for improved self-regulation of nonprofits. Contributing to this important public policy trend was passage of the Sarbanes-Oxley Act of 2002. While passed in response to corporate and accounting scandals, two provisions—pertaining to document destruction and whistleblower protections—also apply to nonprofit organizations (BoardSource and Independent Sector 2006, 2). As another instance of governmental prompting, Senators Chuck Grassley and Max Baucus, in a letter dated September 22, 2004, contacted the president and CEO of Independent Sector, Diana Aviv (Grassley and Baucus 2004). The senators expressed deep concerns about charities exploiting their tax-exempt status, noting the need for legislative remedies to enable good self-regulation. Grassley and Baucus requested Independent Sector to convene a national panel to recommend actions to inform legislative action "that will strengthen good governance, ethical conduct and effective practice of public charities and private foundations" (1). Independent Sector subsequently convened the Panel on the Nonprofit Sector ("the Panel" or "IS Panel"), which issued its Final Report to Congress in June 2005 and a Supplemental Report in April 2006. Nearly 500 organizations and individuals have signed on to the Final Report (Panel on the Nonprofit Sector 2007a) demonstrating strong industry support. Further, many of the Panel's recommendations were enacted into law through the Pension Protection Act of 2006 (IS Panel 2007, 1).

On January 12, 2007, the Panel's Advisory Committee on Self-Regulation of the Charitable Sector issued 29 Draft Principles on Self-Regulation for public comment. The Advisory Committee recommends that all charitable organizations aspire to follow these principles, while all public charities with $1 million or more in annual revenues and private foundations with $25 million or more in assets should implement them (Panel on the Nonprofit Sector 2007c, 1). A second draft with two additional principles was subsequently issued for comment (Panel on the Nonprofit Sector 2007b). In October 2007 the Advisory Committee's final recommendations were issued and expanded to 33 Principles. The principles, designed to promote good governance and ethical practice, are offered to all charitable organizations as guideposts for adopting specific practices that best fit an organization's size and charitable purposes (IS Panel 2007, 6).

Significant progress has clearly occurred in promoting greater understanding of the public need for nonprofit organizations to have increased accountability and improved self-regulation. With the formal endorsement of hundreds of organizations that themselves would be subject to greater accountability, the sector has come far in building consensus for a measurable improvement over the status quo. Furthermore, a solid foundation of principles now exists to guide improved stewardship and self-regulation of all willing organizations of the nonprofit sector.

How will these principles be implemented? As great as the progress achieved so far has been, developing and endorsing principles is just the first step; translating them into practices that can be implemented and documented is quite another. Actions speak louder than words. Very difficult challenges lie ahead: the practical challenges of implementation. Substantial agreement on the destination is now in place; how will nonprofit organizations get there? How will these principles translate into concrete, implementable practices, enforceable at the organizational level? Also, what about cost? Are the principles even economically feasible to implement?

Nonprofit researchers and practitioners have a great opportunity to create strategies and models of implementation, to identify practices and action steps to implement the various principles. Moreover, if strategies emerge that can avoid or at least minimize costs, implementation becomes economically feasible. Rather than merely aspire, small and medium-size nonprofits can put many of these principles in place as well.

Researchers and practitioners can create competing models and strategies of self-regulation to implement the proposed principles. Various researchers have addressed accountability in detail that could prove highly useful to researchers willing to develop strategies and models to implement self-regulatory principles. One example comes from Christensen and Ebrahim (2006), who examined the interplay of accountability and mission. They identify numerous accountability mechanisms and whether accountability is upward, lateral, or downward (Table 1, 199). Young, Bania, and Bailey favor the use of umbrella structures, including accreditation agencies and watchdog groups, among others (1996). Another approach adopts prevention-based solutions, creating new mediating structures and processes at the organizational and sector levels of intervention (Corbett 2000a, 7). Further, structural changes at the state level could promote intersector collaboration, reduce burdensome regulation, and promote more effective service delivery, advancing self-regulation of the sector (Corbett 2001, 6–7).

The purpose here is to identify specific, economically feasible strategies and practices to enable nonprofit organizations of all sizes to successfully incorporate and implement the Principles on Self-Regulation issued by Independent Sector. Second, the approach is structured so nonprofit organizations may proceed to implement immediately any and all principles upon which the organization's stakeholders reach consensus, rather than delay implementation pending full agreement on all principles—a consensus that may prove elusive. The approach taken in this volume attempts to respect and reconcile what may be widely divergent views among stakeholders as to what constitutes improved stewardship and accountability, as seen in prior case study research (Corbett, 2005). Finally, this book is intended for use as a supplement to the Panel's report and should be considered in conjunction with the Panel's proposed principles, background, and rationale, as well as the many citations of applicable legal, legislative, and IRS regulations contained in its report (IS Panel, 2007).

■ OBJECTIVE

The objective of this volume is to encourage partial or full implementation of the 33 Principles on Self-Regulation by identifying specific strategies of implementation, with a bias for prevention, including the Sarbanes-Oxley requirements pertaining to whistleblowing and document destruction (Principles 4 and 5). Second, the recommended approach urges other researchers and practitioners to develop competing models and strategies to provide economically feasible options for all nonprofits willing to improve their stewardship and accountability through self-imposed regulation—advancing organizational, sector, and public-policy needs.

Efforts to develop models and strategies to implement the 33 Principles present a great opportunity to bring together researchers, practitioners, and policymakers, advancing the partnership model (Galaskiewicz 2003). Such efforts should also advance the creation of usable knowledge (Lindblom and Cohen 1979), preferably using simplifying strategies—shortcuts, surrogates, and approximations—because absent strategies, professional inquiry is more blueprint than practice (Lindblom 1990, 269). Further, this presents the opportunity to promote enduring community change by intervening at the highest system levels to achieve second-order change (Heller et al. 1984; Dalton et al. 2001). Successfully translating 33 Principles into practice is a most formidable challenge; empirically based strategies appear to present great opportunity to succeed here.

■ METHOD OF IMPLEMENTATION: PRINCIPLES TO PRACTICE

Pledging allegiance to principle is one thing; living the principle by putting it into practice is something else. While numerous nonprofits have essentially endorsed, or will endorse, many of the Principles on Self-Regulation, no doubt many nonprofits will struggle with integrating such principles into actual practice. How can this be done? While organizations no doubt have many possible ways to attempt implementing the principles, will they be enforceable? Who will enforce compliance? Can compliance be documented, and if so, how?

The approach and strategy proposed here are to translate the principles into practice through the organization's by-laws. Why by-laws? First, all formal nonprofits, regardless of size, have by-laws, so their universality provides a strong starting point. This approach enables small- and medium-sized nonprofits to implement as well. Second, by-laws are the province of the board, which must be involved in crafting each provision and approving it by the required margin. Fashioning and implementing by-laws bring board consensus and the method of board enforcement together at the time of by-law approval, creating a bias for success. Third, by-laws provide a means to examine, expand, and build upon the best practices of other nonprofits. Most of the 33 Principles are not new; many high-performing nonprofits have thoroughly addressed such matters previously.

By-laws may not be the only way to implement the 33 Principles, but this approach has many advantages. The recommendations in this book rely, in part, upon past research conducted in response to many well-publicized nonprofit scandals—research designed to understand, diagnose, and prevent organizational dysfunction (Corbett 1995; 1996) and encourage nonprofit self-regulation (Corbett 1998; 2000a). The recommendations also rely on research designed to prevent board bias in nonprofit organizations (Corbett 2007).

These recommendations translate Independent Sector's 33 Principles on Self-Regulation into practice by devising by-laws for all principles. This step relies in part on a prior survey of A-rated nonprofits that were asked for a copy of their by-laws.[1] Of the 101 nonprofits contacted, 78 responded, resulting in 65 sets of by-laws (Corbett 1996). The by-laws were examined and summarized over many dimensions of governance, including records access, records retention, ethics policy, conflict of interest, disclosure requirements, self-dealing prohibitions, indemnification provisions, mediation provisions, and dissolution provisions (Table 1, 13). Many by-laws directly relate to the 33 Principles on Self-Regulation, presenting an opportunity to tap the collective wisdom of those 65 A-rated nonprofits in developing by-laws that partially or fully implement any of the 33 Principles. More recently, the 65 sets of by-laws were reexamined to address issues related to board composition and board bias (Corbett 2007). That examination resulted in the identification of various additional issues, including term limits, the nomination process, board member qualifications, the board member replacement and removal process, and board development. Many such issues and related by-laws inform the application of the 33 Principles into practice; they were relied upon as well.

The prior by-law research provided guidance or a basis to construct proposed by-laws for implementation. In some cases, a by-law precedent was found to implement the principle, designated B-1 through B-65. In others, a by-law was expanded, or by-laws from multiple nonprofits were combined to more effectively or completely implement the principle. In some cases, a new by-law was constructed. Thus, the method of implementation proposed here is to rely, where possible, on relevant by-laws from A-rated nonprofits, in whole or in part, to implement or advance each principle.[2] This is not to say that every principle is fulfilled completely; that was not always possible. However, each implementing by-law, where it does not fully implement the principle, at least provides incremental progress and a starting point upon which nonprofits can build. This approach enables immediate progress for boards willing to translate the principles into practice.

Many principles are noncontroversial; where so, boards can immediately implement any principles for which board consensus exists. Finally, the by-laws were designed to impose as little incremental cost as possible, or none, enabling small and medium-size nonprofits to implement many of the 33 Principles through their by-laws as well.

Subsequent chapters present each principle, related core issues, a discussion, proposed implementing by-law(s), identification of implementing authority, and a listing of other principles that the proposed by-law supports.[3]

■ NOTES

1. "A-rated" in the sense that they were rated A–, A, or A+ by a national charity rating organization (AIP 1995). The criteria include cost to raise funds, portion of expenses spent on charitable programs, and others. Due to concerns that some respondents expressed, the names of the charities are not shown, with by-laws instead designated from B-1 to B-65.

2. While there was substantial reliance on the referenced material, various changes from the original by-laws (B-1 to B-65) and previously recommended by-laws (Corbett 1996; 2007) were necessary, primarily for consistency of form or to fine tune a proposed by-law to more closely align with the 33 Principles on Self-Regulation. Many of the by-laws recommended here, therefore, were adapted to most effectively advance or implement the 33 Principles. Such modified by-laws are denoted as follows, as appropriate: "(adapted from B-1 to B-65)," "(adapted from Corbett 1996)," and "(adapted from Corbett 2007)." Verbatim quotes from B-1 through B-65 are to the original by-laws (rather than to the excerpt or paraphrase contained in Corbett 1996 and 2007).

3. This reflects the perspective of a researcher/practitioner, not a lawyer. As laws vary by jurisdiction, consultation with appropriate legal counsel is needed to ensure compliance with national, state, and local laws applicable to each organization.

PART 1

Thirty-three Principles for
Good Governance and Ethical Practice
from the Panel on the Nonprofit Sector
Convened by Independent Sector

2

Principles for Legal Compliance and Public Disclosure

■ PRINCIPLE 1

"A charitable organization must comply with all applicable federal laws and regulations, as well as applicable laws and regulations of the states and the local jurisdictions in which it is based or operates. If the organization conducts programs outside the United States, it must also abide by applicable international laws, regulations and conventions that are legally binding on the United States" (IS Panel 2007, 10).

Core Issues

Board orientation/training, staff orientation/training, legal training, restrictions on political activities

Comment

While the principle states that a charitable organization must comply with applicable laws and regulations, for that to be accomplished, board members, executives, and staff all need to be well informed on relevant laws and regulations. This need varies based upon the position and responsibilities of each individual. There is by-law precedent requiring that new board members receive orientation and that educational activities be provided to all board members (B-31; Corbett 2007, 30). This principle can be advanced by specifying that relevant law and regulations should be included and extended beyond board members to executives and general staff. Further, there is by-law precedent for establishing board training responsibility with the nominating committee (B-65; Corbett 2007, 30). Fixing responsibility at the board level through the nominating committee (or if no such committee, where nominating responsibility lies) will help ensure compliance and is recommended here, recognizing that the nominating committee could involve others due to the expansion of training beyond board members. The proposed by-law also adds an annual reporting requirement to help ensure that the board is aware of the degree of compliance, enabling the board to take corrective action, as needed.

Another aspect of this principle that lends itself to a by-law provision or remedy is the prohibition from supporting or opposing candidates for public office or intervening in political campaigns (IS Panel 2007, 11). Many nonprofits may already have such a by-law prohibition. For those without, proposed implementing by-law 1-B is recommended and listed below.

This principle, because of its great breadth, is not easily implemented; however, by-laws 1-A and 1-B should provide incremental progress in furthering Principle 1. Moreover, most of the by-laws proposed to implement the remaining principles further the broad purposes contained under this principle.

Proposed Expanded Implementing By-law(s)

1-A: The board shall take appropriate actions to provide orientation for new directors, executives, and general staff, and annual educational activities for all directors, executives, and general staff. Such orientation and annual education shall include training on federal, state, and local laws and regulations relevant to such employees. The nominating committee will prepare a compliance report and provide it to the board annually.

1-B: The organization shall neither support nor oppose any candidates for public office, nor will the organization intervene in any political campaign in any manner.

Implementing Authority

Nomination committee, board of directors, president

Other Principles Supported

Principle 15

■ PRINCIPLE 2

"A charitable organization should have a formally adopted, written code of ethics with which all of its directors or trustees, staff and volunteers are familiar and to which they adhere" (IS Panel 2007, 12).

■ PRINCIPLE 3

"A charitable organization should adopt and implement policies and procedures to ensure that all conflicts of interest, or the appearance thereof, within the organization and the board are appropriately managed through disclosure, recusal, or other means" (IS Panel 2007, 12).

Core Issues

Ethics policy, conflict of interest, self-dealing, annual disclosure, appearance of impropriety, indemnification of board members, public trust and confidence

Comment

Principles 2 and 3 are addressed together because ethics and conflict of interest issues are integrally related. When addressing ethics and the creation of a written policy, many issues arise, including conflict of interest, disclosure, self-dealing, loans to trustees, and indemnification of board members, to name a few (Corbett 1996, 17–25).

Of the 65 sets of by-laws examined, 11, or 17%, provide for an annual ethics review, and 13, or 20%, contain conflict of interest provisions but without annual review (17). As a result of this prior research, it has been proposed that a best practice is to require disclosure of conflicts on an annual basis, as well as when the conflict arises (18). Further, it has been proposed that adoption of a higher ethics standard than currently exists is needed. That is, adoption of the appearance standard that has the potential to bolster confidence warrants consideration as a best practice for nonprofits that wish to set higher standards than are commonplace inside or outside the Sector (20).

Another related issue is self-dealing. Of the 65 sets of by-laws examined, only 2, or 3%, prohibit self-dealing (18). Many nonprofits, 18, or 28%, allow self-dealing in a qualified way (18). Principle 3 requires that all conflicts of interest, or their appearance, within the organization and board be "appropriately managed through disclosure, recusal or other means" (IS Panel 2007, 12). Thus, the principle does not prohibit self-dealing and appears to allow for it as long as the organization has means to manage it.

At this time, all nonprofits should have a formal ethics policy, and it appears most prudent to prohibit self-dealing to avoid the appearance of impropriety. Moreover, to manage conflicts of interest most effectively, it appears prudent to require annual disclosure of a potential conflict, as well as when one may occur, which has been identified as a recommended best practice previously (Corbett 1996, 18). Implementing by-law 2-A, therefore, contains a requirement for a written ethics policy updated annually; by-law 2-A would also include a prohibition on self-dealing, with disclosure annually, as well as at the time of possible conflict, as previously proposed (20). Recognizing that some boards engage in self-dealing and manage it through disclosure, one less aggressive option than barring self-dealing is to phase it out, as presented in Option 2. A third option is to allow self-dealing and manage it through disclosure, but that still results in an appearance of impropriety and is not recommended here as it stands to undermine public confidence.

Directly related to an ethics policy and conflict-of-interest provision is the issue of indemnification of board members. Based on the review of the 65 sets of by-laws, some nonprofits condition indemnification on ethical behavior by board members, and prohibit self-dealing. A number of by-law precedents exist for conditioning indemnification protection on ethical behavior, especially prohibitions on self-dealing (B-49, B-22, B-60; Corbett 1996, 21). One option for nonprofits is to allow for liberal indemnification if aggressive protections are in place to prohibit self-dealing. This was previously recommended (Corbett 1996, 21–22) and is recommended here, shown as by-law 2-B below. This provision also requires full disclosure as conflicts occur as well as annually, and finally, that approval of indemnification requires a two-thirds vote of all directors. For boards that determine that they do wish to allow self-dealing, they could place aggressive protections such as allowing self-dealing conditioned upon unanimous consent (B-17; Corbett 1996, 19). For a detailed summary and discussion of many by-law requirements of A-rated nonprofits pertaining to ethics, conflict of interest, disclosure, self-dealing, and indemnification, see Corbett 1996 (17–23). For an example of a model code of ethics adopted and recommended by Independent Sector, see Statement of Values and Code of Ethics for Nonprofit and Philanthropic Organizations (IS Accountability 2004).

Proposed Implementing By-law(s):

2-A: Option 1: The board shall establish a written ethics policy, establishing principles and standards of behavior expected of representatives of the organization. The policy shall prohibit material conflicts of interest, including self-dealing, and the appearance of conflicts of interest to the extent practical. Disclosure of such conflicts shall occur at time of awareness and annually through a filing made with the chair. The board shall review and update the policy annually (adapted from Corbett 1996, 20). *(recommended)*

Option 2: The board shall establish a written ethics policy, establishing principles and standards of behavior expected of representatives of the organization. The policy shall prohibit material conflicts of interest, including self-dealing, *prospectively,* and the appearance of conflicts of interest to the extent practical. Disclosure of such conflicts shall occur at time of awareness and annually through a filing made with the chair. The board shall review and update the policy annually (adapted from Corbett 1996, 20). *(less aggressive)*

2-B: The organization will indemnify to the full extent permitted by law against all qualified expenses incurred in the defense of any action entered by reason of the fact that such person is or was a director or officer provided that each (1) abided by the standards of conduct described in by-law 2-A which prohibits self-dealing, and (2) disclosed any conflicts as they occurred as well as on an annual basis by letter filed with the chair of the board. Approval of indemnification requires a concurring vote of two-thirds of all directors (adapted from Corbett 1996, 23). *(recommended)*

Implementing Authority

Chair of the board, board of directors

Other Principles Supported

Principles 1, 2, 6, 7, 12, 15, 18, 20, and 23

▪ PRINCIPLE 4

"A charitable organization should establish and implement policies and procedures that enable individuals to come forward with information on illegal practices or violations of organizational policies. This 'whistle-blower' policy should specify that the organization will not retaliate against, and will protect the confidentiality of, individuals who make good-faith reports" (IS Panel 2007, 14).

Core Issues

Sarbanes-Oxley Act of 2002, "whistleblower" policy, public trust and confidence, prevention, cooperative processes, mediation, alternate dispute resolution (ADR), risk management, whistleblower and ethics training

Comment

This principle requires organizations to establish and implement policies and procedures that enable individuals to come forward with information on illegal practices or violations of organizational policies. Further, this principle requires that the policy specify that the organization will not retaliate and will protect the confidentiality of individuals who act in good faith.

This principle responds to the Sarbanes-Oxley Act of 2002 and seeks to encourage charitable organizations to comply with the legislation. The legislation and principle focus is on institutionalizing corrective action in a primarily reactive and remediative way. That is, the legislation and principle appear designed to put out organizational fires rather than preventing them in the first place. While a provision could be written merely to fulfill the legal obligation, another solution is to instead focus on system-level, prevention-based strategies that still comply with the legal requirement. Such problems can potentially be prevented or remediated with cooperative procedures and process solutions and are recommended here.

One approach to prevention is to prescribe cooperative processes, with prevention potential, in an organization's by-laws. Of the 65 sets of by-laws reviewed, as previously described, four were found to have provisions that introduced cooperative processes to resolve internal conflicts, including mediation and arbitration-type provisions (Corbett 1996, 23–24).

One noteworthy provision authorizes the parent organization to provide assistance to a member. Specifically, the by-law provision empowers the executive committee to authorize another committee to conduct site visits to any member experiencing financial distress. Any one of many circumstances qualify for site-visit assistance, such as a request for a site visit, two consecutive years of operating deficits, failure to file an audited yearly statement, filing a qualified yearly statement, or a situation in which a member is cited for deficiencies by any government agency (B-5). Such a provision helps ensure that the resources and expertise of the parent are provided in a timely fashion to all members, under many conditions, which should help prevent or mitigate grave financial problems, as well as the destructive aftermath that often follows.

Another example that demonstrates an alternative way to ensure the availability and use of cooperative processes, including mediation and arbitration, is as follows:

"The Bylaws of each Organization shall provide for a procedure for the mediation of disputes between the Organization and one or more of its proposed or member Affiliates; in the event that a resolution of the dispute cannot be achieved within ninety (90) days from the receipt by the president of [organization name] of a written notice from the organizers of a proposed Affiliate, or from the Board of Directors of an Affiliate or an Organization of the existence of the dispute, or by agreement sooner, the dispute, together with the names of the persons authorized to act on behalf of the disputants, shall be referred to the [organization name] Board of Directors for final and binding resolution of the [organization name] Board" (B-49; Corbett 1996, 24).

The use of cooperative processes in an organization's by-laws has substantial potential benefit for everyone. The approach proposed here, and given the need to implement Principle 4, is to identify cooperative processes that can be incorporated into an organization's by-laws that will act to encourage cooperative, internal resolutions, potentially eliminating—or at least reducing—problems for which a whistleblower policy may otherwise be needed. Second, mediation and cooperative processes reduce the risk of litigation, which is highly valuable from a risk management perspective. Essentially, this requires developing broader cooperative processes, with prevention potential, directly within the by-laws that still accommodate the requirements of this principle with regard to the establishment of whistleblower policy and procedures.

As the American Bar Association (ABA) notes, mediation is less expensive and faster, and offers a broader range of settlement options than a traditional trial (American Bar Association 2007, 8). The ABA also notes that mediation is a convenient means of resolving many common disputes, including workplace disputes and disputes regarding business matters (7).

It has been previously recommended that nonprofit organizations make a formal and public commitment to explore cooperative processes before considering litigation (Corbett 1996, 23–26). As Henry and Lieberman (1985) describe, many corporations have formally adopted a policy statement, or they take the ADR Pledge (154), where ADR refers to Alternate Dispute Resolution. The purpose is to publicly commit to follow cooperative processes in an effort to avoid litigation. The pledge is nonbinding in that either party may voluntarily pursue litigation if one views that the cooperative approach is not working and a legal resolution is desired. A pioneer advocate for ADR was the Center for Public Resources, a nonprofit corporation founded in New York City, which developed the ADR Pledge. The Center for Public Resources is now called the International Institute for Conflict Prevention and Resolution, or CPR Institute (CPR Annual Report 2006). It is considered the world's leading resource advocating for ADR (1); the Institute has an International Committee on Arbitration (6) and is global in scope, with Advisory Committees in Europe and China (7).

More than 4,000 operating companies have committed to the policy statement for corporations. More than 1,500 law firms—including 400 of the 500 largest firms—have committed to the corresponding version for law firms (ADR Pledge 2007, 1). Two policy statements have been developed, one for corporations and one for law firms wishing to make a formal commitment to explore cooperative processes before pursuing litigation. Those that adopt the ADR Pledge that applies to corporations, which would be most relevant to nonprofit organizations, essentially make a commitment to explore Alternative Dispute Resolution procedures before considering litigation with other parties with whom they do business. By formally adopting the ADR Pledge, companies agree to use collaborative procedures first in an effort to avoid the high costs of litigation; however, either party may proceed with litigation if ADR is unsuitable for the circumstances at hand, or if it fails to produce satisfactory results (ADR Pledge 2010, 1).

Considering its adoption by over 4,000 companies, such a pledge might become even more prevalent and successful with regard to nonprofit organizations from the voluntary sector whose culture should already be relatively biased in favor of cooperative, mediated outcomes (Corbett 1996, 25). In addition to recommending that nonprofit organizations consider taking the ADR Pledge, two by-laws have been developed to implement a cooperative, mediation-based culture within nonprofit organizations (26). Those two provisions were designed to provide mediation options internally, within the organization at the board level, and externally, between the organization and any outside entity. Those provisions incorporate mediation and ADR procedures within the by-laws, listed below as 4-A and 4-B. While Principle 4 does not require introducing a culture of cooperation, doing so will benefit the organization by supporting cooperative processes with prevention potential and helping to prevent and address whistleblower complaints early, before they escalate out of hand. Further, the approach is an effective risk management approach.

Can mediation-type processes be used to prevent or address whistleblower complaints? Yes, by incorporating formal mediation structures or options within the organization's work setting. In describing the many benefits of mediation, the American Bar Association identifies three formal mediation options: a private agency, a workplace ombudsman service, and a community mediation service (American Bar Association 2007, 7). Two options are proposed here for nonprofits to consider in implementing this principle. The first is to institute an ombudsman at the workplace (Option 1). An ombudsman can be an effective intervention for the workplace, and many high-profile companies have adopted this approach (Henry and Lieberman 1985, 109). The second is to institute an ombud panel, which could be done at the sector level. Many advantages exist with an ombud panel, including independence of management, ability to select members with needed expertise, incorporating community interests and values, and providing a valuable complement to the information and resources normally at the board's disposal (Corbett 1998, 26). This option could also be viewed as a community mediation service—relying upon an ombud panel, but implemented at the sector level. Organizations able to afford their own ombud might prefer to have that function dedicated to their organization, such as with Option 1. Medium and smaller size nonprofits with limited or inadequate resources could potentially rely upon sector support, sharing resources and costs.

Alternatively, a substantial sector representative, such as Independent Sector, could potentially arrange pro-bono services for nonprofits willing to implement its proposed principles, including ombud programs to deal with the whistleblower challenge. Pro-bono or discounted services are often associated with the legal profession, as noted in implementing Principle 1 (IS Panel 2007, 10). A similar expectation of IS members, consultants, universities, research organizations, or other sector representatives who could help charities implement these critically important principles—including potentially staffing ombud panels—is reasonable and potentially part of a solution for organizations with inadequate or marginal resources. The clear societal benefits of implementing the 33 Principles at many nonprofit organizations to improve governance and accountability could spur new support for pro-bono services. If Independent Sector is unable to facilitate such a service or function, another potential resource is the CPR Institute, a nonprofit itself, that may be willing to expand its services more broadly to the nonprofit sector. CPR as part of its mission helps resolve complex disputes by devising rules, protocols, and best practices, providing parties with resources and consulting expertise in selecting methods and neutral individuals to assist in dispute resolution (CPR Annual Report 2006, 3).

Both proposed alternatives—using an ombudsman at the organizational level (Option 1) or using an ombud panel at the sector level (Option 2)—are recommended for serious consideration by nonprofits willing to implement Principle 4. Moreover, there appears to be recent, substantive support for the use of ombuds to implement whistleblower protections. According to Jackson and Fogarty, having an ombudsman-type program in place can go a long way to correct problems as they arise and to meet the Sarbanes-Oxley Act requirements (2005, 78; 2006, 150). (Note: for a sample Whistleblower Protection Policy, see Jackson and Fogarty [2005, 189].) Finally, Options 1 and 2 incorporate a requirement that this information be provided annually and in the context of ethics training required annually.

Recommended Implementing By-law(s)

4-A: Board members, upon simple majority vote, may access independent, voluntary, third-party mediation to resolve differences among board members or differences between the board and a chapter, affiliate, or other entity involved with the organization (adapted from Corbett 1996, 26).

4-B: Consistent with our intent to avoid or minimize unnecessary litigation, we will explore Alternate Dispute Resolution (ADR) procedures to resolve differences as shown on the attached Policy Statement, whenever possible in our transactions and dealings with public and private parties. All contracts entered into shall include a clause to reflect our formal commitment to ADR. We will seek, wherever possible, to conduct business with parties willing to make similar commitments (adapted from Corbett 1996, 26).

4-C: Option 1: In response to the Sarbanes-Oxley Act of 2002, the executive committee (if any), in consultation with the president, shall develop an Internal Complaint and Resolution Process (ICRP) available to all staff, volunteers, and clients. The policy shall be designed to allow all such individuals to address and/or report concerns about waste, fraud, abuse, misreporting, or violation of organization rules or policies with the assurance that they will not be retaliated against. The policy shall require the creation of an ombudsman who is a neutral fact finder, authorized to investigate complaints by staff, volunteers, or clients and empowered to talk to anyone in the organization to ascertain facts and make recommendations to senior management, including the board, about resolution, as appropriate. In addition to in-person reporting to the ombudsman, the policy shall also provide three other avenues for communicating such information, including calls to an anonymous hotline, e-mails to a designated account, and submission of reports in writing. The policy will describe how the internal investigation will be conducted, procedures and timeframes for reporting to the board, as well as notification of law enforcement agencies in the case of criminal matters. The policy and complaint activity shall be reviewed by the executive committee (if any) and president on a quarterly basis, with any recommendations or proposed modifications provided to the board for approval, disapproval, or modification. The policy shall be provided to all employees, volunteers, and clients annually, along with the organization's written code of ethics, both addressed in the context of ethics training provided annually. *(recommended)*

Option 2: In response to the Sarbanes-Oxley Act of 2002, the executive committee (if any), in consultation with the president, shall develop an Internal Complaint and Resolution Process (ICRP) available to all staff, volunteers, and clients. The policy shall be designed to allow all such individuals to address and/or report concerns about waste, fraud, abuse, misreporting, or violation of organization rules or policies with the assurance that they will not be retaliated against. The policy shall require the creation of an ombud panel comprising individuals outside the organization who are neutral fact finders, authorized to talk to anyone in the organization to ascertain facts and make recommendations to senior management, including the board, about resolution, as appropriate. In addition to in-person or phone reporting to the ombud panel, the policy shall also provide three other avenues for communicating such information, including calls to an anonymous hotline, e-mail to a designated account, and submission of reports in writing. The policy will describe how the internal investigation will be conducted, procedures and time frames for reporting recommendations to the board, as well as law enforcement agencies in the case of criminal matters. The policy and complaint activity shall be reviewed by the executive committee (if any) and president on a quarterly basis, with any recommendations or proposed modifications provided to the board for approval, disapproval, or modification. The policy shall be provided to all employees, volunteers, and clients annually, along with the organization's written code of ethics, both addressed in the context of ethics training provided annually. *(also recommended)*

Implementing Authority

Executive committee, board of directors, president

Other Principles Supported

Principles 2, 6

■ PRINCIPLE 5

"A charitable organization should establish and implement policies and procedures to protect and preserve the organization's important documents and business records" (IS Panel 2007, 15).

Core Issues

Sarbanes-Oxley Act of 2002, record retention, record destruction, records access, risk management

Comment

Principle 5 requires nonprofits to establish and implement policies and procedures that will protect and preserve important documents and records. As Jacobs noted (1986, 71–76), various state and federal laws require maintaining files, and all associations should develop and follow a record retention program to ensure that necessary records are maintained. It has been recommended that a formal records retention policy appears necessary and that reference to such a policy and requirement within the by-laws is proposed as a best practice (Corbett 1996, 16). More recently, the Sarbanes-Oxley Act of 2002 raises document storage and retention issues that apply to all organizations (Jackson and Fogarty 2005); guidance useful to developing a record retention policy is available (79–84).

Another very important and related issue not addressed in Principle 5 is access to records. This fundamental right to access organizational records is critically important to board members to fulfill their basic governance responsibilities. Further, an access to records by-law stands to be an effective risk management strategy, empowering board members to address issues and concerns before a crisis develops. Organizations lacking a records access officer or function may find such necessary; otherwise it may be implemented via the board's secretary.

Based upon the prior by-law research, which examined 65 sets of by-laws of A-rated organizations, 16 nonprofits, or 25%, provided for trustee access explicitly within the by-laws (Corbett 1996, 15). Following are examples of various record access provisions (15–16):

"All books and records of the Corporation may be inspected by any member or his agent or attorney for any proper purpose at any reasonable time" (B-4).

"Both the Secretary and Treasurer shall permit any member of the Board of Directors or his or her duly authorized attorney to inspect all books and records of [organization name] for any proper purpose at any reasonable time" (B-15).

"Every Director shall have the absolute right at any reasonable time to inspect all books, records, and documents of every kind and the physical properties of the Corporation and each of its subsidiary corporations. This inspection by a Director may be made in person or by an agent or attorney, and the right to inspection includes the right to copy and make extracts of documents" (B-22).

To implement Principle 5, and to address the additional critical issue of a board member's right to records, the following by-laws are proposed here, and were proposed previously (Corbett, 1996, 16). They are listed subsequently as by-laws 5-A and 5-B. While the prior research proposed no specific retention period, three options are proposed below, with four years recommended, assuming the options are not inconsistent with applicable law. An additional by-law requires that the record retention policy be initially developed and reviewed every six months, with any recommendations—whether for change or no change—provided to the board for approval, disapproval, or modification.

Proposed Implementing By-law(s)

5-A: Board members shall have general access and right to review all books, records, plant, and property for any proper purpose, at any reasonable time. Written requests for copies of records shall be made to the secretary and shall be provided within 30 days. This includes, but is not limited to, memoranda, financial reports, audits, expense records, itemized legal costs, and contracts (adapted from Corbett 1996, 16).

5-B: The books and records shall only be destroyed in accordance with a written record retention policy that describes the various records and required holding periods (adapted from Corbett 1996, 16). [Insert option]

> Option 1: The minimum holding period is three years.
> *(least aggressive)*
> Option 2: The minimum holding period is four years.
> *(recommended)*
> Option 3: The minimum holding period is five years.
> *(most aggressive)*

5-C: The executive committee (if any) and president shall provide the record retention policy to the board for approval, disapproval, or modification, with a subsequent review every six months thereafter, providing a report to the board with recommendations for continuation or revision, for board approval, disapproval, or modification.

Implementing Authority

Records access officer, president, secretary, board of directors

Other Principles Supported

Principles 3, 4, 6, 7, 8, 15, and 21

■ PRINCIPLE 6

"A charitable organization's board of directors should ensure that the organization has adequate plans to protect its assets—its property, financial and human resources, programmatic content and material, and its integrity and reputation—against damage or loss. The board should review regularly the organization's need for general liability and directors' and officers' liability insurance, as well as take other actions necessary to mitigate risks" (IS Panel 2007, 16).

Core Issues

Risk management, preservation of organizational assets, indemnification, dissolution policy, litigation risk, public trust and confidence

Comment

Various precedents protecting organizational assets were found. A common one protects nonprofit assets in the event of dissolution. Of the 65 sets of by-laws examined, 22, or 34%, contained a dissolution provision (Corbett 1996, 26). Alternatively, some nonprofits are silent on dissolution and fail to provide any process to ensure all surviving assets are redirected to an equivalent charitable purpose. Failure to address this critically important matter exposes the organization to dissolution with no board-approved process in place. According to Oleck and Stewart (1994, 1567), provisions for dissolution and distribution should be in the by-laws. Considering that the board is responsible for managing the resources of the nonprofit, it appears imperative that all nonprofits explicitly address the future dissolution of the corporation within their by-laws (Corbett 1996, 27). Further, for a nonprofit in crisis, possibly headed to protracted litigation, dissolution can salvage resources that may otherwise be headed down the drain of litigation (Corbett 1995, 30). Such a provision has been proposed as a best practice that creates an avenue for graceful nonprofit demise (Corbett 1996, 27). It is also prudent to establish that in no event may surviving assets be transferred to benefit any past or present board members. Dissolution provision 6-A should provide incremental progress in advancing Principle 6.

Another exposure to loss of organizational assets occurs when board members or other individuals depart, resign, or are terminated. There is by-law precedent for providing protection by requiring the return of all assets at departure (B-58; Corbett 2007, 26). By-law provision 6-B achieves such protection and is recommended as an implementing by-law.

Generally, this principle requires attention to risk management, an approach furthered by creating a board-level compliance and reporting function. For those without such a function already assigned, such as to an audit committee, implementing by-law 6-C is proposed. This by-law will help ensure board-level attention to compliance with all governing instruments, by-laws, board-approved policies, and board-level reporting requirements. Alternatively, such responsibility could go to a board member or existing committee.

With regard to the periodic review of an organization's need for general liability and directors' and officers' liability insurance, the proposed implementing by-law specifies such review annually. Because it is related to indemnification provided under Principle 2 and by-law 2B, the proposed implementing by-law is designated 2-C below.

More frequent board meetings are proposed as a risk management strategy, as incorporated under proposed implementing by-law 8-A, addressed subsequently. Bimonthly or quarterly meetings (Options 1 and 2, respectively) should present the organization lower risk than less frequent meetings. Monthly would be more aggressive yet. A second risk management strategy in by-law 8-A is to require 45-day advance notice of proposed board meetings, along with at least a 15-day notice of the draft agenda, with a board member's right to propose additional agenda items. This strategy should significantly increase board member awareness of upcoming decisions, as well as provide for an explicit opportunity to raise any concerns in advance of a board meeting, by incorporating them into the meeting agenda. By-law 8-A describes these recommended requirements.

Proposed Modified Implementing By-law(s)

6-A: Board members shall have, where consistent with applicable law, the right to dissolve the organization and redirect all remaining net assets to two or more existing nonprofits having the same or similar purpose, determined and approved by a two-thirds vote of all members of the board, ratified by majority vote of the membership, where applicable. In no event may assets be transferred to the direct or indirect benefit of an existing or past board member (adapted from Corbett 1996, 27).

6-B: Any and all representatives entrusted with any books, records, or property of the organization shall maintain and keep such in good order, at the appropriate office of the organization and have them available for authorized audit, examination, or inspection at all times. All officers and directors at the end of their terms or when removed or when their office is declared vacant shall deliver to their duly appointed successors, or board chair, all books, papers, monies, and other property assigned to them or in their possession belonging to the organization, and they shall not be relieved from their bonds or obligations until they have so complied (adapted from B-58; Corbett 2007, 26).

6-C: To further the organization's risk management, the board shall have a Compliance Committee (or equivalent) responsible for monitoring internal compliance with all governing instruments, including the by-laws, all board-approved policies, and all board-level reporting requirements. The Committee shall provide a quarterly report to the board, indicating whether deficiencies exist and, if so, proposed remedies for board approval, disapproval, or modification.

2-C: The board shall review, at least annually, the organization's need for general liability and directors' and officers' liability insurance and implement such changes, if any, it deems necessary to manage such risks.

Implementing Authority

Board of directors, membership (if any)

Other Principles Supported

Principles 2, 5, and 8

■ PRINCIPLE 7

"A charitable organization should make information about its operations, including its governance, finances, programs, and activities, widely available to the public. Charitable organizations also should consider making information available on the methods they use to evaluate the outcomes of their work and sharing the results of those evaluations" (IS Panel 2007, 17).

Core Issues

Records access policy, public access to information, evaluation methods and results, public trust and confidence

Comment

Principle 7 requires public access to information about operations, governance, finances, programs, and activities. Second, the principle encourages organizations to provide public access to methods used to evaluate outcomes of their work and the evaluation results.

The first requirement raises the question of public versus proprietary records, which is related to Principle 5. The records access policy should include not only specific determinations of holding periods for various records, as required by 5-B, but also determinations as to which records are public versus proprietary. This determination warrants board consultation with counsel familiar with state and federal laws that may impact holding periods and privacy issues that may vary with type of nonprofit and mission. As the records are examined to determine the proper holding period(s), a determination can be made as to whether they are public documents based on legal and policy decisions. Which governance, finance, and other records it makes public can be described in its record retention policy. This step is appropriate because any public requests for documents—whether by media, elected officials, members of the general public, or any other stakeholders—will require reference to the record retention policy, which describes even whether such documents exist. There is precedent in by-laws for providing public access to records, at nominal charge, as follows:

"The records, books, and annual reports of the financial activities of the Corporation shall be kept at the principal office of the Corporation in the State of _____ for at least three years after the closing of each fiscal year and shall be available to the public for inspection and copying there during normal business hours. The Corporation may charge for the reasonable expense of preparing a copy of a record or report" (B-33; Corbett 1996, 16).

Principle 7 may be implemented by building upon, and referencing, the written record retention policy required in by-law 5-B, proposed in 7-A below.

The second requirement raised in Principle 7 is that nonprofits are encouraged to make evaluation methods available to the public—a step that can be readily implemented for nonprofits with written evaluation methods, which many nonprofits likely already have. Those nonprofits without methods need to develop them. While challenging, measurable evaluation criteria can be developed and may vary widely depending on the organization's mission, goals, programs, and values. Yet evaluation methods, tools, and criteria can be created (Corbett 2000b, 341–44); developing written criteria and methods for those without it is needed to implement this aspect of Principle 7. By-law 7-B is proposed below.

The third aspect of Principle 7 pertains to evaluation results. Some results, depending on what is evaluated and the findings, may fall within the proprietary area. As a result, an organization will need to have a process to assess, and determinations would likely have to be made on a case-by-case basis, by the board, as reflected in 7-C.

Regarding the method of making information public, for efficiency, access, and cost reasons, public information can go on a website or be provided upon request, as reflected below.

Proposed Implementing By-law(s)

7-A: In the organization's written record retention policy, for each record and holding period determined, there shall be a determination as to whether the record qualifies as proprietary or not, and therefore, subject to public access. This policy shall be reviewed and updated by the records access officer, or an individual assigned the records access role, and provided annually for board approval, disapproval, or modification.

7-B: The organization shall incorporate such information into its existing public record access policy (or, where lacking, develop one) that describes the process of requesting public records and the methods and conditions for public inspection and copying, such as through web access and/or in-person request at specified locations, and costs, if any, of preparing such information for release.

7-C: Evaluation Methods: Evaluation methods used by the organization shall be in the form of a written policy and shall be periodically reviewed and updated and provided annually to the board for review. Such evaluation methods shall generally be considered public, consistent with the record retention policy, and posted on the organization's website or available upon request. Evaluation results shall be made public on a case-by-case basis, upon individual request, or on the organization's website, at board discretion.

Implementing Authority

Records access officer, president, board of directors

Other Principles Supported

Principles 5, 6, 18, 19, and 24

3

Principles for Effective Governance

"A charitable organization must have a governing body that is responsible for reviewing and approving the organization's mission and strategic direction, annual budget and key financial transactions, compensation practices and policies, and fiscal and governance policies" (IS Panel 2007, 20).

Core Issues

Board oversight, annual budget approval, compensation review and approval, policy oversight, meeting frequency, board member communication and participation

Comment

This principle conveys the board's general oversight responsibility for review and approval of mission, strategic direction, annual budget, key financial transactions, compensation practices and policies, as well as the fiscal and governance policies of the organization. The by-laws reviewed lacked significant guidance for implementing this principle. However, various provisions can be devised to implement it. While not stated explicitly here, along with the budget review process, a periodic review of income, including portfolio performance, is needed, as it may dictate adjustments to approved expenditures, either upward or downward. Thus, portfolio performance review has been added to the implementing by-law. Additionally, this is an opportune provision to address board meeting frequency and board participation in the process to enable effective oversight. Given widespread access to electronic media, highly cost-effective means now exist to facilitate board participation to improve board oversight and governance. While boards can create alternatives, three options on the number of meetings per year are proposed: bimonthly, quarterly, or semiannually, with quarterly meetings recommended here. To help promote board understanding and participation, a 45-day notice for meetings is proposed, along with notice of 15 days for the draft agenda. To enable greater participation and oversight, the provision allows directors to add items to the proposed agenda. Due to the wide use and efficiency of electronic media, meeting in person is required only annually, as proposed below.

Proposed Implementing By-law

8-A: Throughout the year and at its periodic meetings, the board shall be responsible for reviewing and approving the mission and strategic direction, annual budget and key financial transactions, compensation practices and policies, and fiscal and governance policies of the organization. In the context of its budget review and monitoring of actual performance, the board shall also review the performance and prudence of the investment portfolio so that adjustments to the budget or portfolio may be made periodically as needed. As part of its oversight and monitoring of compensation, the board will hire, oversee, and annually evaluate the performance of the chief executive officer. It will also approve, annually, any adjustment beyond cost of living, or if within one year of the expiration of an existing contract, where applicable, the level of compensation, including all benefits.

> Option 1: The board shall meet bimonthly. *(most aggressive)*
> Option 2: The board shall meet quarterly. *(recommended)*
> Option 3: The board shall meet semiannually. *(least aggressive)*

(Add to Option 1 or 2 or 3) The board shall have at least one meeting per year that is face-to-face, with the remaining meetings being in person, via teleconference or videoconference, or a combination thereof. Board members shall receive notice from the secretary at least 45 days in advance of a proposed meeting, in writing by standard mail or electronically via fax or e-mail. The secretary shall provide a copy of the draft agenda at least 15 days in advance, in the same form, with board members free to propose additional agenda items. The board shall be free to delegate such matters as described above to any applicable subcommittee(s) as long as their recommendations are documented and similarly provided in advance of such meetings, for board approval, disapproval, or modification.

Implementing Authority

Secretary, board subcommittee(s), board of directors, president

Other Principles Supported

Principles 6, 9, 13, and 22

▓ PRINCIPLE 9

"The board of a charitable organization should meet regularly enough to conduct its business and fulfill its duties" (IS Panel 2007, 21).

Core Issues

Board meeting frequency, risk management

Comment

As described under Principle 8, three options are proposed for meeting frequency: bimonthly, quarterly, or semiannually, with quarterly recommended here. More frequent meetings should constitute a risk management strategy that is related to Principle 6. See the Principle 8 Comment for further explanation. Proposed implementing by-law 8-A also implements Principle 9.

Proposed Implementing By-law
  See Principle 8, By-law 8-A

Implementing Authority

Secretary, board subcommittee(s), board of directors

Other Principles Supported

Principles 6, 8, 13, and 22

■ PRINCIPLE 10

"The board of a charitable organization should establish its own size and structure and review these periodically. The board should have enough members to allow for full deliberation and diversity of thinking on governance and organizational matters. Except for very small organizations, this generally means that the board should have a minimum of five members" (IS Panel 2007, 21).

Core Issues

Annual self-assessment, board size and structure, board composition, board diversity

Comment

This principle requires the board to establish its own size and structure, and to review this periodically, noting that the board should be large enough for full deliberation and diversity of thinking on governance and other matters. Such an activity could readily be incorporated into a self-assessment process and/or retreat process so as to address this periodically, such as described by Chait, Holland, and Taylor (1996, 32–47). Unfortunately, no frequency is specified in the principle. There is by-law precedent for a one-year requirement; the board must provide a process for annual self-evaluation of the board (B-31; Corbett 2007, 30). This precedent appears most aggressive. Three options— most aggressive, aggressive, and least aggressive—are listed, with the middle option recommended here.

The second issue raised in this principle is board size, with five members as a minimum, except for very small organizations. The nonprofit literature is mixed on board size; clearly, board size will vary depending on many factors. Specifying a general floor of five with some flexibility is consistent with this principle, with individual boards best suited to determine an actual greater floor, if desired, and preferably a ceiling as well.

Proposed Expanded Implementing By-law

10-A: Option 1: Duties and responsibilities of the board include providing a process for an annual self-evaluation of the board that includes reviewing its size and structure, along with policies and procedures on term length and limits, to ensure effective governance, and to meet organizational goals and objectives. The minimum board size shall be five members. *(most aggressive)*

Option 2: Duties and responsibilities of the board include providing a process for a self-evaluation of the board once every two years that includes reviewing its size and structure, along with policies and procedures on term length and limits, to ensure effective governance, and to meet organizational goals and objectives. The minimum board size shall be five (or more) members, and the ceiling shall not exceed X. *(recommended)*

Option 3: Duties and responsibilities of the board include providing a process for a self-evaluation of the board once every three years that includes reviewing its size and structure, along with policies and procedures on term length and limits, to ensure effective governance, and to meet organizational goals and objectives. The minimum board size shall be five members. *(least aggressive)*

Implementing Authority

Board of directors

Other Principles Supported

Principles 11, 16, and 17

■ PRINCIPLE 11

"The board of a charitable organization should include members with the diverse background (including, but not limited to, ethnic, racial, and gender perspectives), experience, and organizational and financial skills necessary to advance the organization's mission" (IS Panel 2007, 22).

Core Issues

Board member qualifications, board composition and diversity, nomination process, committee service requirements, board member replacement process, public trust and confidence

Comment

There is by-law precedent for innovative provisions that establish expectations of board members and that promote board diversity (Corbett 2007, 18). Various by-laws require consideration of various specific qualities in the selection process for prospective nominees to the board (B-52, 55; Corbett 2007, 18) while another establishes an annual process whereby the board, when it considers new nominees, has a report on the existing makeup of the board (B-7; Corbett 2007, 18). This process enables the board to take into consideration the current makeup of the board so it can be factored into the board's current decision-making process and rectify any perceived deficiencies. That is, the by-law provides the board with an opportunity to promote greater board balance and diversity as it assesses and selects from the various nominees. The first provision recommended below, 11-A, is a combination of two, each noted by the original by-law's designation, with the addition of the requirement of financial literacy, as required by Principle 11. The provision extends promoting diversity beyond the board to staff by requiring that the president submit an annual report to the board.

Another by-law provision can further the experience and expertise requirement of Principle 11. There is by-law precedent where committee service is a qualifying factor or condition for board service (B-6, B-37; Corbett 2007, 30). This would significantly further Principle 11 as it spurs board members to either self-select or be selected for more specific roles. For example, by-law B-37 (Corbett 2007, 30) requires all board members to serve on at least two committees. Some degree of committee service should effectively tap special talents and unique skills of board members and further advance the organization's mission. This appears a reasonable expectation that would further Principle 11 and is recommended below as 11-B.

Another obligation of this principle is for the board to make sure that it is equipped with the experience to fulfill its responsibilities. Board vacancies occur for many reasons, and organizations are vulnerable to circumstances often out of their control, including illness, death, and other unforeseen circumstances. Some organizations have innovative provisions that facilitate the board member replacement process, such as by-law B-62, which ensures that recommendations come from the nominating committee (Corbett 2007, 23), rather than result from a more restricted or chaotic process. Other organizations provide for a contingency plan in case the nominations do not occur, such as by-law B-42 (Corbett 2007, 23), which should help prevent or avoid prolonged vacancies that could grow over time and seriously undermine board functioning. The last by-law recommended here, 11-C, combines those two provisions.

Proposed Expanded Implementing By-law(s) 11-A, 11-B, and 11-C

11-A: The NC (Nominating Committee or equivalent) shall evaluate and recommend candidates for the board and all committees. In evaluating candidates, consideration shall be given to (1) organizational needs, (2) board balance and diversity, (3) leadership ability, (4) availability to serve, and (5) other factors the board may specify, including financial literacy (adapted from B-55; Corbett 2007, 18).

The NC, when submitting nominations, shall also report on the makeup of the board with respect to gender, race, and nationality. Diversity shall also be considered in staff recruitment, and the president shall report annually to the board on the makeup of the staff (adapted from B-7; Corbett 2007, 18).

11-B: It is board policy that all members will serve on at least one board committee, which the NC shall consider when qualifying and selecting candidates to most effectively meet board needs (adapted from B-6, B-37; Corbett 2007, 30).

11-C: The board shall fill all vacancies caused by resignation, removal, or death of any officer, board member, or NC member upon recommendation of the NC. Any board vacancies caused by resignation, removal, death, or other reason and not filled by the board within 10 days may be filled by executive committee majority vote on an interim basis until the next annual or other special meeting (adapted from B-42, B-62; Corbett 2007, 22).

Implementing Authorities

Nomination committee, president, executive committee, board

Other Principles Supported

Principles 1, 6, 10, and 15

■ PRINCIPLE 12

A substantial majority of the board of a public charity, usually meaning at least two-thirds of the members, should be independent. Independent

members should not: (1) be compensated by the organization as employees or independent contractors; (2) have their compensation determined by individuals who are compensated by the organization; (3) receive, directly or indirectly, material financial benefits from the organization except as a member of the charitable class served by the organization; or (4) be related to (as a spouse, sibling, parent or child), or reside with any individual described above" (IS Panel 2007, 23, footnote omitted).

Core Issues

Board independence, nomination process, disqualification standards, board member removal process, nominations outside the board, public trust and confidence

Comment

In satisfying this principle, it becomes necessary to assess and evaluate prospective board members who are under consideration for nomination. For the nominating committee to develop a slate of candidates and present them to the board only to learn later that some candidates had disqualifying traits would be a waste of resources. Therefore, incorporating these criteria into the standards or disqualifying standards of potential board members is an effective way to proceed. Few organizations specify disqualification standards in by-laws, a point that is also related to board member removal standards. One example is a by-law provision that allows for removal of a board member for conviction of a felony (B-1) or for conviction of a crime of moral turpitude (B-30; Corbett 2007, 21). An example of a disqualifying standard is by-law B-44, which prohibits service of an individual with a background in intelligence work (Corbett 2007, 21). One need raised by placing various requirements on board member nominees is that it creates a significant time demand in examining and evaluating potential candidates. Further, it places a new burden on those approving such nominations to make sure that none of the various disqualifying standards apply, individually or as a group.

Some nonprofits have well-thought-out nomination processes that provide for a nomination process with specific time frames and filing requirements to ensure that adequate time and notice are provided to evaluate candidates. While many boards have no written processes or procedures (Corbett 2007, 15), some do, as outlined in by-laws B-3 and B-33 (Corbett 2007, 14). For the purposes of implementing Principle 12, an expansion of by-law B-33 appears sufficient to capture the independence standard and potentially disqualifying traits, and is recommended here.

Proposed Modified Implementing By-law

12-A: The NC (or equivalent) shall nominate directors, officers, committee chairs, and committee members as follows:

1. The chair of the NC shall solicit nominations for directors, officers, committee chairs, and committee members from each director and officer, including the president, at least 90 days prior to the annual meeting of the board. Nominations, with biographical information, are due to the EC chair no later than 75 days prior to the meeting (adapted from B-33; Corbett 2007, 14).

2. The NC shall consider the nominations submitted and submit the NC's list of all persons nominated, together with their biographical information, to the secretary for inclusion in the 60-day notice of annual meeting. The 60-day notice shall also inform the directors that nominations for directors, officers, committee chairs, and committee members accompanied by biographical information may be entertained from the floor at the annual meeting, subject to NC certification that the director nominees, in aggregate with the existing members, would not violate the independence standard noted below (adapted from B-33; Corbett 2007, 14).

3. With regard to existing board composition and prospective board nominees, if approved, a substantial majority of the board, at least two-thirds (2/3) should be independent. They should be individuals (1) who are not compensated by the organization as an employee or independent contractor; (2) whose compensation is not determined by individuals compensated by the organization; (3) who do not receive, directly or indirectly, material financial benefits from the organization except as a member of the charitable class served by the organization; and (4) who are not related to (as a spouse, sibling, parent, or child), or do not reside with, any individual described above (adapted from IS Panel 2007, 23, Principle 12).

Implementing Authority

Nomination committee, board of directors

Principles 10, 11, and 14

■ PRINCIPLE 13

"The board should hire, oversee, and annually evaluate the performance of the chief executive officer of the organization, and should conduct such an evaluation prior to any change in that officer's compensation, unless there is a multi-year contract in force or the change consists solely of routine adjustments for inflation or cost of living" (IS Panel 2007, 24).

Core Issues

Executive compensation, performance evaluation

Comment

Principle 13 requires the board to hire, oversee, and annually evaluate the performance of the chief executive officer as well as approve annually, and in advance, that compensation unless there is a multiyear contract in force or the change consists of a cost-of-living adjustment. This principle was addressed under Principle 8; see its comment for further explanation. Proposed implementing by-law 8-A, listed here, also implements Principle 13.

Note: While not explicitly addressing benefits, this principle has been added below to make it clear that consideration of compensation must include and reflect all benefits.

Proposed Implementing By-law

8-A: Throughout the year and at its periodic meetings, the board shall be responsible for reviewing and approving the mission and strategic direction, annual budget, key financial transactions, compensation practices and policies, and fiscal and governance policies of the organization. In the context of its budget review and monitoring of actual performance, it shall also review the performance and prudence of the investment portfolio so adjustments to the budget or portfolio may be periodically made, as needed. As part of its oversight and monitoring of compensation, the board will hire, oversee, and annually evaluate the performance of the chief executive officer. The board will also approve, annually, any adjustment beyond cost of living, or if within one year of the expiration of an existing contract, where applicable, the level of compensation, including all benefits.

Option 1: The board shall meet bimonthly. *(most aggressive)*
Option 2: The board shall meet quarterly. *(recommended)*
Option 3: The board shall meet semiannually.
    (least aggressive)

(Option 1 or 2 or 3) The board shall have at least one meeting per year that is face-to-face, with the remaining meetings being in person, teleconference or videoconference, or a combination thereof. Board members shall receive notice from the secretary at least 45 days in advance of a proposed meeting, in writing by standard mail or electronically via fax or e-mail. The secretary shall provide a copy of the draft agenda at least 15 days in advance, in the same form, with board members free to propose additional agenda items. The board shall be free to delegate such matters as described above to any applicable subcommittee(s) as long as their recommendations are documented and similarly provided in advance of such meetings, for board approval, disapproval, or modification.

Implementing Authority

Secretary, board subcommittee(s), board of directors

Other Principles Supported

Principles 8, 9, and 22

▨ PRINCIPLE 14

"The board of a charitable organization that has paid staff should ensure that the positions of chief executive officer, board chair, and board treasurer are held by separate individuals. Organizations without paid staff should ensure that the positions of board chair and treasurer are held by separate individuals" (IS Panel 2007, 27).

Core Issues

Board independence, role conflict, board composition, conflict of interest, disqualification standards, board member removal process, public trust and confidence

Principle 14, which avoids conflicting roles, is also related to Principle 12. For organizations with paid staff, Principle 14 requires that separate individuals hold the positions of chief executive officer, board chair, and treasurer. This requires that chief executive officers not be nominated into those positions and that individuals sitting in those positions give up those positions, if selected as chief executive officer. These disqualification and removal provisions would readily fit as an addition to by-law 12. As most nonprofits have paid staff, the proposed by-law assumes such. (*Note:* Organizations without paid staff can relax the provision accordingly, limiting the restriction only to board chair and treasurer roles, consistent with Principle 14's intent.) Implementing by-law 12-B is proposed to satisfy Principle 14 requirements and is listed subsequently. *Note: This principle specifies that the individuals shall not be the same but fails to address the "related party" disqualification contained in Principle 12. In furtherance of Principle 12, "related party" has been added to proposed by-law 12-B, as described here.*

Proposed Implementing By-law

12-B: In order to preserve board independence, and to avoid conflicting duties or interests, the positions of chief executive officer, board chair, and board treasurer shall be held by separate and unrelated individuals, as defined in 12-A. Therefore, in the selection of potential nominees to the board, by the NC or any other nominators, any individual in the position of chief executive officer shall not qualify for nomination to such other positions. In the event that a sitting board chair or treasurer is appointed chief executive officer, that individual shall resign his or her chair or treasurer board position, on or before the effective date of said appointment. Absent such resignation, the secretary shall notify that individual in writing of his or her removal from the board chair or treasurer role, effective no later than the effective date of the new appointment. This provision does not bar continuation of board membership in other new or open board roles, as deemed appropriate and approved by the board.

Nominating committee, secretary, board of directors

Other Principles Supported

Principles 11 and 12

■ PRINCIPLE 15

"The board should establish an effective, systematic process for educating and communicating with board members to ensure that they are aware of their legal and ethical responsibilities, are knowledgeable about the programs and activities of the organization, and can carry out their oversight functions effectively" (IS Panel 2007, 28).

Core Issues

Board member orientation and training, legal training, ethics and whistleblowing policy training, committee service

Comment

This principle was largely addressed under the recommended by-laws implementing Principles 1, 4, and 11 (as noted here). Implementing by-laws for Principles 1 and 4 provide for legal, ethics, and whistleblowing policy training annually. This should address awareness of legal and ethical responsibilities of all employees, including board members. Implementing by-laws 1-A and 4-C (Option 1) are listed subsequently. With regard to promoting knowledge about programs and activities, by-law 11-B, listed here, requires service on one or more committees that should have the effect of increasing familiarity with the organization's programs and activities, particularly if committee service is rotated among board members periodically.

Proposed Implementing By-law(s)

1-A: The board shall take appropriate actions to provide for orientation for new directors, executives, and general staff, and annual educational activities for all directors, executives, and general staff. Such orientation and annual education shall include training on federal, state, and local laws and regulations relevant to such employees. A compliance report will be prepared by the NC and provided to the board annually.

4-C: Option 1: In response to the Sarbanes-Oxley Act of 2002, the executive committee (if any), in consultation with the president, shall develop an Internal Complaint and Resolution Process (ICRP) available to all staff, volunteers, and clients. The policy shall be designed to allow all such individuals to address or report concerns about waste, fraud, abuse, misreporting, or violation of organization rules or policies with the assurance that they will not be retaliated against. The policy shall require the creation of an ombudsman who is a neutral fact finder, authorized to investigate complaints by staff, volunteers, or clients, and empowered to talk to anyone in the organization to ascertain facts and make recommendations to senior management, including the board, about resolution, as appropriate. In addition to in-person reporting to the ombudsman, the policy shall also provide three other avenues for communicating such information including calls to an anonymous hotline, e-mails to a designated account, and submission of reports in writing. The policy will describe how the internal investigation will be conducted, procedures and time frames for reporting to the board, as well as notification of law enforcement agencies in the case of criminal matters. The policy shall be reviewed by the executive committee (if any) and president on a quarterly basis, with any proposed modifications provided to the board for approval, disapproval, or modification. The policy shall be provided to all employees, volunteers, and clients annually, along with the organization's written code of ethics, both addressed in the context of ethics training provided annually.

11-B: It is board policy that all members will serve on at least one board committee, which the NC shall consider when qualifying and selecting candidates to most effectively meet board needs (adapted from B-6, B-37; Corbett 2007, 30).

Implementing Authority

Nominating committee, board of directors

Other Principles Supported

n/a

■ PRINCIPLE 16

"Board members should evaluate their performance as a group and as individuals no less frequently than every three years, and should have clear

procedures for removing board members who are unable to fulfill their responsibilities" (IS Panel 2007, 28).

Core Issues

Individual and full board self-assessment, board member removal process, meeting attendance: policy and removal

Comment

This is related to Principle 10, where the implementing by-law provides for a self-evaluation every one, two, or three years, with the two-year option recommended. Any of the three options would satisfy the minimum three-year requirement contained in Principle 16. To add the individual assessment, 10-A has been revised accordingly. Recommended by-law 10-A revised (option 2) is cited here.

With regard to policies and procedures on board member removal, various issues are raised. There is significant precedent here as some boards have addressed this in substantial detail within their by-laws; the provisions and processes vary widely (Corbett 2007, 23–30). Many differences exist regarding ease of removal, method, standards for removal, notice requirements, and hearing rights. Many precedents and examples of by-law provisions exist with regard to removal with or without cause (B-35, 10, 19), removal with cause (B-13, 33), removal with hearing rights (B-18, 3, 57), automatic removal for meeting absences (B-50, 35, 62), as well as various innovative provisions (B-54, 27, 58, 34, 7; Corbett 2007, 23–25).

For the purposes of implementing this principle, a combination of two provisions is recommended. The recommendation specifies a removal process for specified acts, with a right to notice and hearing before the board (B-57; Corbett 2007, 24), as well as an attendance policy, specifying a process initiated by the Nominating Committee (NC), with its basis and recommendations, for final action by the board (B-7; Corbett 2007, 25). (*Note:* Since the by-law precedent, B-57, did not specify a length of time for board member reply, a 30-day requirement has been added. Second, a requirement has been added that the board member response be made in writing so that the full board may carefully consider the response. It is noted here as 16-A.)

Proposed Expanded Implementing By-law(s)

10-A (rev.): Duties and responsibilities of the board include providing a process for a self-evaluation of the board (*and individual members*) once every two years, which includes reviewing its size and structure, along with policies and procedures on term length and limits, to ensure effective governance and to meet organizational goals and objectives. The minimum board size shall be five (or more) members and shall not exceed [insert number here]. (Option 2)

16-A: Removal Process: Officers and directors may be removed by a two-thirds (2/3) board vote for two or more unexcused absences, by-law violation, misconduct, neglect of duty, or behavior detrimental to the organization. Before such action is taken, the individual(s) must be advised of specific charges, given reasonable time of at least 30 days to prepare a written response, and afforded a full hearing before the board (adapted from B-57; Corbett 2007, 24).

Attendance Policy: Directors are expected to attend board meetings on a regular basis and may be removed if they fail to meet this standard. In the month after the last meeting of the year, the secretary shall forward to the NC the names of directors who missed all such meetings that year. Each case shall be reviewed by the NC, considering any other contributions made to the organization and individual circumstances like business or personal emergencies. Prior to the next board meeting, the NC shall recommend, based on majority vote, whether each director shall be removed, warned, or retained and the reasons for the recommendation. The board may accept, modify, or reject NC recommendations (adapted from B-7; Corbett 2007, 25).

Implementing Authority

Nominating committee, board of directors

Other Principles Supported

Principles 7 and 9

■ PRINCIPLE 17

The board should establish clear policies and procedures setting the length of terms and the number of consecutive terms a board member may serve" (IS Panel 2007, 29).

Core Issues

Board structure, term length, term limits

Comment

This is related to Principle 10 that requires periodic board review of the board's size and structure, including consideration of policies and procedures on term length and limits. Recommended by-law 10-A satisfies this principle.

Proposed Implementing By-law

10-A (rev.): Duties and responsibilities of the board include providing a process for self-evaluation of the board (*and individual members*) once every two years that includes reviewing its size and structure, along with policies and procedures on term lengths and limits, to ensure effective governance and to meet organizational goals and objectives. The minimum board size shall be five (or more) members and the ceiling shall not exceed [insert number here]. (Option 2)

Implementing Authority

Board of directors

Other Principles Supported

n/a

◼ PRINCIPLE 18

"The board should review organizational and governing instruments no less frequently than every five years" (IS Panel 2007, 30).

Core Issues

Organizational policies, conflict-of-interest policies, code of ethics, record retention policy, whistleblower policy, articles of incorporation, by-law review and update

Comment

Principle 18 requires that organizational and governing instruments be reviewed no less frequently than every five years. This would include all policies, including conflict-of-interest, code of ethics, record retention, and whistleblower policies, as well as the articles of incorporation and the by-laws. Three options are proposed here—at two years, three years, and five years, with three years the recommended frequency. One development acting to increase the need for more regular board review is passage of the Sarbanes-Oxley legislation as updates or revisions to the law may occur that would impact nonprofits. Moreover, if that legislation is further expanded, nonprofits must be capable of reacting quickly to ensure compliance with the law. Second, more frequent reviews would further Principle 6, which requires boards to engage in risk management practices. More frequent review, coupled with greater board participation in the affairs of the nonprofit, stands to reduce risks to the organization.

Proposed Implementing By-law

18-A: Option 1: The board shall review, and update as needed, all organizational and governing instruments, including its conflict-of-interest, ethics, record retention, and whistleblower policies, articles of incorporation, and by-laws no less frequently than every two years. *(most aggressive)*

Option 2: The board shall review, and update as needed, all organizational and governing instruments, including its conflict-of-interest, ethics, record retention, and whistleblower policies, articles of incorporation, and by-laws no less frequently than every three years. *(recommended)*

Option 3: The board shall review, and update as needed, all organizational and governing instruments, including its conflict-of-interest, ethics, record retention, and whistleblower policies, articles of incorporation, and by-laws no less frequently than every five years. *(least aggressive)*

Implementing Authority

Board of directors

Other Principles Supported

Principles 1, 3, 4, 5, 6, 8, and 10

■ PRINCIPLE 19

"The board should establish and review regularly the organization's mission and goals and should evaluate, no less frequently than every five years,

the organization's programs, goals, and activities to be sure they advance its mission and make prudent use of its resources" (IS Panel 2007, 30).

Core Issues

Mission review, program evaluation, prudency

Comment

While other principles involve periodic board meetings and reviews for specified purposes (Principles 8, 10, 16, and 18), this principle requires review of the mission and evaluation of the organization's programs, goals, and activities. Due to the magnitude and importance of the requirement, it is recommended as justifying its own stand-alone provision. Moreover, changes resulting from this activity have potentially wide-range impacts on the future of the organization. The five-year minimum contained in the principle appears to be on the long side, and a shorter period of no less often than every three years is proposed here. Further, some organizations, depending upon economics and funding decisions, may wish to expand this provision to require an independent, professional program evaluation to inform board review and decision making. Due to the scope and potential costs of implementing this principle, an option for a more frequent requirement than once every three years for an evaluation is not proposed here, but with an annual review requirement by the board of the organization's goals in implementing the mission. The implementing by-law 19-A is proposed as described here.

Proposed Implementing By-law

19-A: The board will establish and review goals for implementing the organization's mission on an annual basis and evaluate once every three years the organization's programs, goals, and activities to ensure that they advance the mission and make prudent use of resources.

Implementing Authority

Board of directors

Other Principles Supported

Principles 8, 10, 11, 15, and 24

■ PRINCIPLE 20

"Board members are generally expected to serve without compensation, other than reimbursement for expenses incurred to fulfill their board duties. A charitable organization that provides compensation to its board members should use appropriate comparability data to determine the amount to be paid, document the decision and provide full disclosure to anyone, upon request, of the amount and rationale for the compensation" (IS Panel 2007, 31).

Core Issues

Pro-bono service, board member compensation, conflict of interest, public trust and confidence, expense reimbursement

Comment

Principle 20 establishes the general expectation that directors serve the nonprofit on a pro-bono basis. The principle provides that any exceptions should be justified based on comparability data, with the decision documented. Further, such organization should provide full disclosure to anyone, upon request, of the amount(s) and rationale.

A further bolstering of this principle can be achieved by clarifying that the expense must be reasonable and by requiring annual board review and approval of compensation beyond expenses. Both are recommended here. Three options are proposed reflecting increasing levels of board approval, with unanimous board approval the option recommended here. By-law 20-A is proposed to implement this principle.

Proposed Implementing By-law

20-A: Compensation of board members, beyond reimbursement of reasonable expenses incurred in connection with board responsibilities, is prohibited. Exceptions to this provision must be supported by comparable data, with the level of compensation and rationale publicly available, upon request.

Option 1: Second, such compensation must be annually reviewed and approved by unanimous vote of the board of directors. *(recommended)*

Option 2: Second, such compensation must be annually reviewed and approved by a two-thirds vote of the board of directors. *(aggressive)*

Option 3: Second, such compensation must be annually reviewed and approved by a majority vote of the board of directors. *(least aggressive)*

Implementing Authority

Board of directors

Other Principles Supported

Principles 3, 8, 9, and 23

4

Principles for
Strong Financial Oversight

■ **PRINCIPLE 21**

"A charitable organization must keep complete, current, and accurate financial records. Its board should receive and review timely reports of the organization's financial activities and should have a qualified, independent financial expert audit or review these statements annually in a manner appropriate to the organization's size and scale of operations" (IS Panel 2007, 34).

Core Issues

Record maintenance and retention, records access, reporting requirements, annual financial audit, risk management, public trust and confidence, public access

Comment

The maintenance and retention of records is addressed under proposed by-laws 5-A, 5-B, and 5-C. Those implementing by-laws address board members' rights to access (5-A), record retention and destruction (5-B), and record retention policy approval and update (5-C), as shown here. These by-laws support implementation of Principle 21. Principle 21 also requires the board to receive and review timely reports of financial activities and an annual financial audit, completed by an independent financial auditor and in a manner appropriate to the size and scale of the organization. By-law 21-A is proposed to satisfy this requirement. Larger organizations may wish to specify additional monthly or quarterly reporting requirements. A quarterly reporting requirement is reflected here, under the responsibility of the chief financial officer, in furtherance of the Principle 22 requirement that the full board review and approve the annual budget and monitor actual performance against the budget. While no public access is required, Principle 7 requires making financial information widely available to the public, and as a result, a web publication requirement has been added here.

Proposed Implementing By-law(s)

5-A: Board members shall have general access and right to review all books, records, plant, and property for any proper purpose, at any reasonable time. Written requests for copies of records shall be made to the secretary and shall be provided within 30 days. These records include, but are not limited to, memoranda, financial reports, audits, expense records, itemized legal costs, and contracts (adapted from Corbett 1996, 16).

5-B: The books and records shall only be destroyed in accordance with a written record retention policy that describes the various records and required holding periods (adapted from Corbett 1996, 16). [Insert Option]

> Option 1: The minimum holding period is three years.
> *(least aggressive)*
> Option 2: The minimum holding period is four years.
> *(recommended)*
> Option 3: The minimum holding period is five years.
> *(most aggressive)*

5-C: The executive committee (if any) and president shall provide the record retention policy to the board for approval, disapproval, or modification, with a subsequent review every six months thereafter, providing a report to the board with recommendations for continuation or revision, for board approval, disapproval, or modification.

21-A: An independent financial report or audit will be prepared annually and submitted to the board of directors for examination and review. The board shall also receive quarterly reports of the organization's financial activities, conducted under the authority of the chief financial officer. Such reports shall be filed with the secretary within 45 days of the close of each calendar quarter. The board shall determine, considering the recommendations of the chief financial officer and president, what financial information should be made generally available to the public through posting on the organization's website.

Implementing Authority

Chief financial officer, president, secretary, board of directors

Other Principles Supported

Principles 5, 7, 8, 15, and 22

■ PRINCIPLE 22

"The board of a charitable organization must institute policies and procedures to ensure that the organization (and, if applicable, its subsidiaries) manages and invests its funds responsibly, in accordance with all legal requirements. The full board should review and approve the organization's annual budget and should monitor actual performance against the budget" (IS Panel 2007, 35).

Core Issues

Financial oversight, portfolio monitoring, budget review and approval, monitoring performance against budget

Comment

Principle 22 requires the board to institute policies and procedures to ensure that the organization manages and invests its funds responsibly in accordance with all legal requirements. The principle also states that the full board should review and approve the organization's annual budget and should monitor actual performance against the budget.

Proposed by-laws 8-A and 21-A contain various reporting requirements that provide for regular board review of investments and annual budget against performance that satisfy the requirements of Principle 22. These requirements are shown here.

Many organizations vest responsibility for investments and finances with a subcommittee, which is an option for boards. Alternatively, this function could be performed by the full board, which would require that it regularly monitor performance throughout the year, including monitoring actual performance against the budget. This latter approach has been incorporated within the proposed implementing by-law 8-A, developed for Principle 8. Boards that wish to further implement Principle 22 could delegate to a subcommittee and do so by adding a provision requiring the subcommittee to perform a periodic assessment with budget or portfolio recommendations, as needed, providing it to board members on a quarterly basis for board approval, disapproval, or modification.

Proposed Implementing By-law(s)

8-A: Throughout the year and at its periodic meetings, the board shall be responsible for reviewing and approving the mission and strategic direction, annual budget and key financial transactions, compensation practices and policies, and fiscal and governance policies of the organization. In the context of its budget review and monitoring of actual performance, the board shall also review the performance and prudence of the investment portfolio so that adjustments to the budget or portfolio may be made periodically as needed. As part of its oversight and monitoring of compensation, the board will hire, oversee, and annually evaluate the performance of the chief executive officer. It will also approve, annually, any adjustment beyond cost of living, or if within one year of the expiration of an existing contract, where applicable, the level of compensation, including all benefits.

Option 1: The board shall meet bimonthly. *(most aggressive)*
Option 2: The board shall meet quarterly. *(recommended)*
Option 3: The board shall meet semiannually. *(least aggressive)*

(Add to Option 1 or 2 or 3) The board shall have at least one meeting per year that is face-to-face, with the remaining meetings being in person, via teleconference or videoconference, or a combination thereof. Board members shall receive notice from the secretary at least 45 days in advance of a proposed meeting, in writing by standard mail or electronically via fax or e-mail. The secretary shall provide a copy of the draft agenda at least 15 days in advance, in the same form, with board members free to propose additional agenda items. The board shall be free to delegate such matters as described above to any applicable subcommittee(s) as long as their recommendations are documented and similarly provided in advance of such meetings, for board approval, disapproval, or modification.

21-A: An independent financial report or audit will be prepared annually and submitted to the board of directors for examination and review. The board shall also receive quarterly reports of the organization's financial activities, conducted under the authority of the chief financial officer. Such reports shall be filed with the secretary within 45 days of the close of each calendar quarter. The board shall determine, considering the recommendations of the chief financial officer and president, what financial information should be made generally available to the public through posting on the organization's website.

Implementing Authority

Secretary, board subcommittee(s), board of directors, chief financial officer, president

Other Principles Supported

n/a

■ PRINCIPLE 23

"A charitable organization should not provide loans (or the equivalent, such as loan guarantees, purchasing or transferring ownership of a residence or office, or relieving a debt or lease obligation) to directors, officers or trustees" (IS Panel 2007, 37).

Core Issues

Ethics, self-dealing, appearance of impropriety, conflict of interest, executive compensation, public trust and confidence

Comment

This principle avoids problems such as the appearance of impropriety and a form of self-dealing by prohibiting loans, or their equivalents, to directors, officers, and trustees. While there is no explicit prohibition for loans to related persons or persons resided with that could present a means of circumventing the intent of this principle, such prohibition has been added, relying upon the definition of "related persons" as contained in Principle 12. By-law 23-A implements this principle and also furthers implementation of Principles 12 and 20 that discourage, restrict, or generally prohibit compensation of board members beyond expenses incurred in the performance of their duties.

Proposed Implementing By-law

23-A: All directors, officers, and trustees are prohibited from receiving loans, transfers of property, release of debt or lease obligations, or any similar forms of financial benefit. Such prohibitions also apply to a spouse, sibling, parent, or child, as well as any person residing with said employee. (See "related person" definition contained in Principle 12.)

Implementing Authority

Board of directors

Other Principles Supported

Principles 3, 12, and 20

■ PRINCIPLE 24

"A charitable organization should spend a significant percentage of its annual budget on programs that pursue its mission. The budget should also provide sufficient resources for effective administration of the organization, and, if it solicits contributions, for appropriate fundraising activities" (IS Panel 2007, 38).

Core Issues

Budget approval, industry standards and benchmarks, excessive costs, public trust and confidence

Comment

This provision requires that a significant percentage of the annual budget be spent on programs that advance the mission and that the budget provide sufficient resources for administration and fundraising. This principle is directly related to Principle 8, which addresses the board's review and approval of the annual budget, as well as fiscal policies of the organization. One way to implement this principle is for the board to consider these issues at the time of its deliberations and budget approval, as is recommended here.

More specifically, this principle can be implemented through a by-law requirement that provides the board with relevant information to make informed judgments as the board considers approving, disapproving, or modifying the proposed budget. Recognizing that this principle does not identify specific benchmarks to be applied generically, benchmarks can still be developed, tailored to an individual organization by individuals familiar with its particular structure, mission, and goals. This approach should be helpful to a board in making informed judgments about each area at the time the budget is proposed, reviewed, modified, or approved. Proposed benchmarks, coupled with historic experience for the organization, should provide very helpful guidance and guideposts to boards not only in the annual budget process but also in comparing their performance to other like organizations, and implementing board prerogatives over time.

To illustrate such standards, the Better Business Bureau has identified standards for charity accountability (BBB Wise Giving Guide 2009, 48) directly related to implementing this principle. Criteria it adopts include a floor of 65% for program activities and a cap on fundraising expenses of 35% of related contributions (48). Organizations that do not wish to adopt a generic benchmark, along the lines of the BBB criteria, can develop their own and adopt by board resolution, using and updating the approved standards over time, as needed, to gauge reasonableness and monitor favorable or unfavorable trends. This approach avoids being bound by generic criteria that may not be appropriate for the organization. The finance committee or its equivalent would be well suited to this responsibility of identifying recommended benchmarks and for providing recent historic experience, along with any related recommendations, to guide the board's decision making. By-law 24-A reflects a by-law provision to implement this principle.

Proposed Implementing By-law

24-A: As part of the annual budget review and approval process, the finance committee (or equivalent) will provide the board with recommended benchmarks including for overall program expense, administrative costs, and fundraising costs, with basis, and how they compare to amounts contained in the current budget request or proposal. The report shall also include the latest five years of comparable historic data to assist in its budget deliberations, along with any related recommendations for the current budget proposal(s).

Implementing Authority

Board subcommittee(s), board of directors

Principles 6, 8, 21, and 22

■ PRINCIPLE 25

"A charitable organization should establish clear, written policies for pay-
ing or reimbursing expenses incurred by anyone conducting business or
traveling on behalf of the organization, including the types of expenses
that can be paid for or reimbursed and the documentation required. Such
policies should require that travel on behalf of the organization is to be un-
dertaken in a cost-effective manner" (IS Panel 2007, 39).

Core Issues

Expense reimbursement, reasonable and necessary expenses, excessive
compensation, public trust and confidence

Comment

Principle 25 requires the establishment of clear expense reimbursement
policies and that expenses should be incurred and reimbursed in a cost-
effective manner. This provision is clearly designed to avoid or prevent
the kinds of abuses that have been highly publicized in the media.

As previously noted by the Panel, federal per-diem expense reimbursement rates can be a useful guide, but there are limitations and circumstances
where reimbursement at such rates is not reasonable or possible (Panel on
the Nonprofit Sector 2007a, 37). Further, the Panel notes that government
employees may have access to discounted rates not currently available to
charitable organizations (37).

Expense reimbursement involves subjective factors and creates difficult
challenges. Organizations should have a written travel expense reimbursement
policy that is reviewed and updated regularly, preferably at least annually.
This policy is recommended here as an element of the proposed implementing by-law. Also, while there are impediments to using federal per-diem
rates, various options could overcome those challenges, particularly considering that federal per-diem rates are updated periodically and established by
geographic area, and are publicly available. Allowing modest premiums over
the federal allowance could allow for satisfaction of the principle's primary

goal to avoid lavish reimbursements while still providing reasonable expense reimbursement. Three options are proposed here to substantially implement Principle 25.

Proposed Implementing By-law

25-A: The organization shall establish a written Expense Reimbursement Policy that applies to the organization's board members, officers, staff, consultants, volunteers, and others traveling on behalf of the organization. The policy shall preclude or restrict the use of premium or first-class travel unless it can be shown to be in the best interest of the organization, as well as prohibit reimbursement of travel expenses for spouses, dependents, or others not conducting business on behalf of the organization. Such a policy shall be consistently applied and transparent to board members and other traveling staff. The policy should reflect requirements and restrictions applicable under current law and prohibit personal employee use. The policy should be reviewed and updated annually and provided to the board for approval. The policy should also provide that all expenses will be reimbursed based upon documentation of actual expenses incurred by the traveler while on organization business, except that they shall not exceed federal per-diem rates, applicable for the location of travel, by more than [a stated percentage].

Option 1: 15% *(most aggressive)*
Option 2: 25% *(recommended)*
Option 3: 35% *(least aggressive)*

Implementing Authority

Board of directors, chief financial officer, president

Other Principles Supported

Principles 6, 8, 12, 13, 15, 18, 19, and 20

■ PRINCIPLE 26

"A charitable organization should neither pay for nor reimburse travel expenditures for spouses, dependents, or others who are accompanying someone conducting business for the organization unless they, too, are conducting such business" (IS Panel 2007, 40).

Core Issues

Reimbursement restrictions, public trust and confidence

Comment

Principle 26 is addressed by proposed implementing by-law 25-A, which prohibits expense reimbursement for spouses, dependents, or others not conducting organization business.

Proposed Implementing By-law

25-A: The organization shall establish a written Expense Reimbursement Policy that applies to the organization's board members, officers, staff, consultants, volunteers, and others traveling on behalf of the organization. The policy shall preclude or restrict the use of premium or first-class travel unless it can be shown to be in the best interest of the organization, as well as prohibit reimbursement of travel expenses for spouses, dependents, or others not conducting business on behalf of the organization. Such a policy shall be consistently applied and transparent to board members and other traveling staff. The policy should reflect requirements and restrictions applicable under current law and prohibit personal employee use. The policy should be reviewed and updated annually and provided to the board for approval. The policy should also provide that all expenses will be reimbursed based upon documentation of actual expenses incurred by the traveler while on organization business, except that they shall not exceed federal per-diem rates, applicable for the location of travel, by more than [a stated percentage].

> Option 1: 15% *(most aggressive)*
> Option 2: 25% *(recommended)*
> Option 3: 35% *(least aggressive)*

Implementing Authority

Board of directors, chief financial officer, president

Other Principles Supported

n/a

5

Principles for
Responsible Fundraising

■ PRINCIPLE 27

"Solicitation materials and other communications addressed to donors and the public must clearly identify the organization and be accurate and truthful" (IS Panel 2007, 42).

Core Issues

Public trust and confidence, truth in advertising, risk management

Comment

This principle requires accurate and truthful communication with donors and the public. A small mistake here can cause great damage to the integrity and reputation of the organization, undermining public trust and confidence. It could also trigger costly litigation and damage the public trust. From a risk management perspective, the magnitude of the risks justifies multiple levels of review of all solicitation scripts, ads and fundraising letters, and outreach. Internal staff or outside contractors, or a combination of the two, can create such material; all such products should be subject to review and approval, as described here. In the event there is no resource and fundraising committee (or its equivalent), the full board should review and approve the material. The following by-law is proposed to implement this principle.

Proposed Implementing By-law

27-A: The organization is committed to fully accurate and truthful communications with all donors and the general public. All solicitation materials, scripts, ads, fundraising letters, or other such outreach—whether prepared internally by staff or by outside contractors—shall be reviewed by the president and subject to approval, disapproval, or modification by the resource and fundraising committee (or its equivalent). All such approved solicitation material shall be posted or otherwise available to the board of directors at least 30 days prior to publication or issuance.

Implementing Authority

President, resource and fundraising committee (or the equivalent), board of directors

Other Principles Supported

Principles 1, 6, and 28

■ PRINCIPLE 28

"Contributions must be used for purposes consistent with the donor's intent, whether as described in the relevant solicitation materials or as specifically directed by the donor" (IS Panel 2007, 43).

Core Issues

Donor trust and confidence, truth in advertising, risk management

Comment

This principle requires that donor intent be respected. Yet conditions change over time, which creates circumstances that may warrant apparent modification of the use of funds. Misunderstandings between donors and organizations can result in protracted and expensive litigation, as well as damage the reputation and public perception of a charity. As a result, it is recommended that any deviations from donor intent be forwarded to the board for evaluation. Because of the potentially serious consequences to the organization, it is recommended that the board be informed and render a decision, with the decision requiring unanimous board consent. While this is aggressive, it is done so in furtherance of protecting the organization's assets, integrity, and reputation, as further required by Principle 6. By-law 28-A implements this principle.

To further implement this principle, and strengthen the concept that funds will be applied consistent with donor intent, another by-law provision is recommended that requires further modification to proposed by-law 6-A. As discussed previously under Principle 6, there is need for a specific provision that addresses the disposition of assets, at the end of the organization's life. Due to the strong basis for having a dissolution provision, as previously described, this provision is ripe for modification to explicitly protect donor intent. Moreover, if there were a time when the risk of failure to respect donor intent was greatest, it would appear at the end of an organization's life, a time often accompanied by great conflict and chaos. Yet boards can establish their commitment to respect donor intent, through the entire organizational life, by adding such a provision and explicit requirement to a dissolution provision, as recommended here in by-law 6-A (revised). Donor intent can, and should, be protected and preserved to the maximum extent possible through the dissolution process, even to the extent of dictating non-profit recipients.

Proposed Implementing By-law(s)

28-A: All contributions will be used consistent with the purpose(s) described in applicable solicitation materials or as specified by the donor. Any deviations from the donor intent conveyed at the time of donation shall require written approval by the donor, or donor's legal representative, and be provided to the board for acceptance or rejection.

> Option 1: Acceptance requires unanimous approval of the board. *(recommended)*
> Option 2: Acceptance requires two-thirds approval of the board. *(less aggressive)*
> Option 3: Acceptance requires majority approval of the board. *(least aggressive)*

6-A (rev.): Board members shall have, where consistent with applicable law, the right to dissolve the organization and redirect all remaining net assets to two or more existing nonprofits having the same or similar purpose, determined and approved by a two-thirds (2/3) vote of all members of the board, ratified by majority vote of the membership, where applicable. In no event may assets be transferred to the direct or indirect benefit of an existing or former board member (adapted from Corbett 1996, 27).

Proposed Addition

This dissolution provision shall not be used to circumvent donor intent nor does it relieve the organization of its obligation to honor the intent of all current and prior donors where funds have been received by the organization for designated purpose(s).

Implementing Authority

Board of directors

Other Principles Supported

Principles 6, 27, and 30

■ PRINCIPLE 29

"A charitable organization must provide donors with specific acknowledgments of charitable contributions, in accordance with IRS requirements, as well as information to facilitate the donors' compliance with tax law requirements" (IS Panel 2007, 44).

Core Issues

Compliance with IRS requirements, facilitating donor compliance, public and donor trust and confidence, risk management

Comment

Principle 29 requires that the organization provide its donors with specific acknowledgments of their contributions and provide information to facilitate compliance with tax law requirements. While detailed internal procedures may exist to implement this principle, to increase or further bolster satisfaction of the principle, the obligation and commitment could be added to the promotional materials that

Principle 27 addresses. Further, as a way to provide information to facilitate donors' compliance with tax law requirements, the promotional materials can incorporate the name of an appropriate contact person or position with a phone number or e-mail address who would be accountable and responsible to facilitate a prompt response. That is, these organizational commitments can be instituted publicly and incorporated as statements included in the outreach effort. Principle 29 can be implemented with a further addition to proposed by-law 27-A, listed here as proposed by-law 27-B. Also, proposed by-law 27-B further supports Principle 27, which requires that solicitation materials clearly identify the organization, by virtue of its requirement that the name and number of a representative of the organization be stated in the solicitation materials or other outreach effort. Finally, the review and approval process involving the president, resource and fundraising committee (or equivalent), and board of directors required in by-law 27-A should help ensure that Principles 27 and 29 are fully implemented.

Proposed Implementing By-law(s)

27-A: The organization is committed to fully accurate and truthful communications with all donors and the general public. All solicitation materials, scripts, ads, fundraising letters, or other such outreach—whether prepared internally by staff or by outside contractors—shall be reviewed by the president and subject to approval, disapproval, or modification by the resource and fundraising committee (or its equivalent). All such approved solicitation material shall be posted or otherwise available to the board of directors at least 30 days prior to publication or issuance.

27-B: The organization shall convey its commitment to provide donors with specific acknowledgments of contributions, in accordance with IRS requirements, and to facilitate donor compliance with tax law requirements by, first, including such a statement within all solicitation and outreach materials referred to above and, second, providing the appropriate name or position and contact information to whom related inquiries may be directed for prompt reply.

Implementing Authority

President, resource and fundraising committee (or equivalent), board of directors

Other Principles Supported

Principle 27

■ PRINCIPLE 30

"A charitable organization should adopt clear policies, based on its specific exempt purpose, to determine whether accepting a gift would compromise its ethics, financial circumstances, program focus, or other interests" (IS Panel 2007, 45).

Core Issues

Public trust and confidence, conflict of interest, risk management

Comment

This principle has no explicit criteria and is highly subjective, yet implementation of the principle is exceedingly important as it relates to risk management; failure to implement this principle could expose the organization to expensive and protracted litigation or result in substantial damage to its reputation. One option, recommended here, is for donations that come with obligations or strings—as compared to undesignated donations or for board-approved, designated uses—be forwarded to the board for its evaluation and approval or rejection. While this may appear an extreme remedy, the risks appear substantial, financially and from a public trust standpoint. Moreover, while it is tempting to recommend that a minimum dollar threshold be established, that is not recommended here. Even small donations can create large appearance problems, as some relatively small contributions to political candidates that ultimately get returned to donors so illustrate. By-law provision 30-A is proposed to implement this principle. Three options are illustrated for the threshold for board approval, with the recommendation that unanimous board approval be required for acceptance of questionable donations. While again this provision is aggressive, it is done so in furtherance of protecting the organization's assets, integrity, and reputation, as further required by Principle 6. Moreover, with today's proliferation of electronic communication, resolving such matters can be expedited with minimal burden on board members with the right procedures in place.

Proposed Implementing By-law

30-A: The organization will not accept donations that undermine, or are inconsistent with, its mission or goals; compromise its ethics or financial circumstances; or are otherwise deemed harmful. Any donations or gifts that constitute funds for designated purposes, other than for designated purposes preapproved by the board, shall be immediately reported and forwarded by the president to the board for evaluation and action to accept or reject such donation. [Option]

> Option 1: Acceptance of the donation requires unanimous approval of the board. *(recommended)*
> Option 2: Acceptance of the donation requires two-thirds (2/3) approval of the board. *(less aggressive)*
> Option 3: Acceptance of the donation requires majority approval of the board. *(least aggressive)*

Implementing Authority

President, board of directors

Other Principles Supported

Principles 6, 24, and 28

■ PRINCIPLE 31

"A charitable organization should provide appropriate training and supervision of the people soliciting funds on its behalf to ensure that they understand their responsibilities and applicable federal, state, and local laws, and do not employ techniques that are coercive, intimidating or intended to harass potential donors" (IS Panel 2007, 46).

Core Issues

Staff orientation and training, contractor training and supervision, public and donor trust and confidence, organization integrity and reputation

Comment

This principle requires that appropriate training and supervision be provided to all people soliciting funds on behalf of the organization. Because it is a training requirement, it lends itself to be implemented in tandem with proposed by-law 1-A (shown here), which also addresses training, including related legal issues. This principle also relates to Principle 6, which requires that risks be managed and the reputation and integrity of the organization be protected. Due to the high risk associated with this activity—regarding the organization's integrity and reputation and the potential risks of not complying with applicable law—the by-law is structured to involve board-level implementation. This principle is also related to Principle 27, which requires solicitation material and other communications with donors to be accurate and truthful. Principle 27 provides a review and approval process involving the president and resource and fundraising committee. This requirement should be incorporated into the training process as well. Finally, the proposed by-law adds a reporting requirement to verify compliance annually with the board by incorporating such information into the reporting requirement contained in proposed by-law 1-A. Proposed by-law 1-C implements this principle, as described here.

Proposed Implementing By-law(s)

1-A: The board shall take appropriate actions to provide orientation for new directors, executives, and general staff, and annual education activities for all directors, executives, and general staff. Such orientation and annual education shall include training on federal, state, and local laws and regulations relevant to such employees. The nominating committee will prepare a compliance report and provide it to the board annually.

1-C: The board shall take appropriate actions to provide, or arrange in coordination with staff, appropriate training and supervision of all people soliciting funds on its behalf to ensure that they understand their responsibilities and applicable federal, state, and local laws, and do not employ techniques that are coercive, intimidating, or intended to harass potential donors. This requirement applies not only to internal staff but also to any outside contractors selected to raise funds on behalf of the organization. The training shall also inform participants of the need for all solicitation materials and outreach to be reviewed and approved, as required in by-law 27-A, applicable to staff and outside contractors. The nominating committee will include a summary of any such training delivered during the year in its annual compliance report to the board, referred to above.

Implementing Authority

Nominating committee, board of directors, president

Other Principles Supported

Principles 1, 6, and 27

■ PRINCIPLE 32

"A charitable organization should not compensate internal or external fundraisers based on a commission or a percentage of the amount raised" (IS Panel 2007, 47).

Core Issues

Preventing coercive practices, public and donor trust, risk management

Comment

This principle prohibits the use of commission or percentage compensation for internal and external fundraisers. This commitment to the public and donors can be made publicly by including such information or a pledge on solicitation materials or other outreach efforts. Another reason for publicizing such a prohibition is that it could have the effect of bolstering public and donor trust and confidence in nonprofits willing to make such a pledge. Moreover, by including it as a requirement within the material itself, it is self-implementing and subject to the review and approval process contained in the by-laws 27-A and 27-B implementing Principles 27 and 29, listed here. Proposed by-law 27-C implements this prohibition on commission reimbursement as outlined here. Further, the solicitation materials or outreach should include the statement that any concerns about the content of solicitation materials or the use of high-pressure tactics should be promptly reported to a representative of the organization to alert it and provide opportunity to promptly investigate and address the concerns, if needed. These proposed by-laws mitigate risk to the organization and represent valuable elements of a risk management plan.

Proposed Implementing By-law(s)

27-A: The organization is committed to fully accurate and truthful communications with all donors and the general public. All solicitation materials, scripts, ads, fundraising letters, or other such outreach—whether prepared internally by staff or by outside contractors—shall be reviewed by the president and subject to approval, disapproval, or modification by the resource and fundraising committee (or its equivalent). All such approved solicitation material shall be posted or otherwise available to the board of directors at least 30 days prior to publication or issuance.

27-B: The organization shall convey its commitment to provide donors with specific acknowledgments of contributions, in accordance with IRS requirements, and to facilitate donor compliance with tax law requirements by, first, including such a statement within all solicitation and outreach materials referred to above and, second, providing the appropriate name or position and contact information to whom related inquiries may be directed for prompt reply.

27-C: The organization shall convey its aversion and opposition to the use of high-pressure tactics by fundraisers and commits to the public and its donors that it will not allow either internal or external fundraisers to be compensated on a commission or percentage basis of funds raised, by including such a statement within its solicitation and outreach materials. Second, to provide a vehicle for reporting high-pressure or other questionable practices, such solicitation materials shall provide the name or position and number of a representative.

Implementing Authority

President, resource and fundraising committee (or its equivalent), board of directors

Other Principles Supported

Principles 6 and 27

■ PRINCIPLE 33

"A charitable organization should respect the privacy of individual donors and, except where disclosure is required by law, should not sell or otherwise make available the names and contact information of its donors without providing them an opportunity at least once a year to opt out of the use of their names" (IS Panel 2007, 48).

Core Issues

Privacy rights, public and donor trust and confidence

Comment

This principle can effectively be implemented along with Principles 27, 29, and 32 as it similarly reflects a commitment to donors and needs to be widely conveyed. Further, these prior principles have an established review process involving the president, resource and fundraising committee (or its equivalent), and board of directors, which can be readily used with little or no incremental burden. The organization can publicize its public commitment to protecting donor privacy by including such information directly within its solicitation and related material. The prior by-laws 27-A, 27-B, and 27-C—implementing Principles 27, 29, and 32—are noted here, along with the proposed by-law 27-D, which expresses the organization's commitment to protect the privacy of its donors. Taken together, the proposed by-law implementation of these four principles should provide significant incremental risk management to help protect the integrity and reputation of the organization, as well as avoid or mitigate various risks of litigation stemming from donor solicitation and outreach activities conducted by, or for, charitable organizations.

Proposed Implementing By-law(s)

27-A: The organization is committed to fully accurate and truthful communications with all donors and the general public. All solicitation materials, scripts, ads, fundraising letters, or other such outreach—whether prepared internally by staff or by outside contractors—shall be reviewed by the president and subject to approval, disapproval, or modification by the resource and fundraising committee (or its equivalent). All such approved solicitation material shall be posted or otherwise available to the board of directors at least 30 days prior to publication or issuance.

27-B: The organization shall convey its commitment to provide donors with specific acknowledgments of contributions in accordance with IRS requirements, and to facilitate donor compliance with tax law requirements by, first, including such a statement within all solicitation and outreach materials referred to above and, second, providing the appropriate name or position and contact information to whom related inquiries may be directed for prompt reply.

27-C: The organization shall convey its aversion and opposition to the use of high-pressure tactics by fundraisers and commits to the public and its donors that it will not allow either internal or external fundraisers to be compensated on a commission or percentage basis of funds raised, by including such a statement within its solicitation and outreach materials. Second, to provide a vehicle for reporting high-pressure or other questionable practices, such solicitation materials shall provide the name or position and number of a representative.

27-D: The organization shall convey its commitment to protect the privacy of its donors by not selling or otherwise making available such names and contact information, except as may be required by law, absent donor approval with the right to opt out at least annually, by including such a statement within all solicitation and outreach materials referred to above.

Implementing Authority

President, resource and fundraising committee (or equivalent), board of directors

Other Principles Supported

Principles 6 and 27

PART 2

Putting Principles into Action

6

Accountability and Enforcement

To summarize, to implement the 33 Principles on Self-Regulation, 38 by-laws are proposed. This is fewer than anticipated; two or more by-laws for each principle would not be unexpected. A single by-law provision can be constructed to advance multiple, or even many, other principles, as can be seen from the *Other Principles Supported* section of each by-law, which shows that one or two by-laws often support three, four, five, or even up to nine other principles. For example, by-laws 2, 5, 7, 8, 18, 19, 20, 24, and 25 support many Principles on Self-Regulation. A single well-constructed by-law has the potential to support, or implement, multiple principles. These proposed by-laws may warrant particular attention by boards seeking to create the most powerful implementing by-laws.

Turning now to accountability and enforcement, several observations are in order. First, as noted, 38 implementing by-laws are proposed. How were they constructed to promote accountability and enable enforcement? This is accomplished in part with reporting requirements to give the board critical information to help inform its decision-making processes. Implementation has internal costs, as reporting requirements place incremental burdens on line or executive staff, board committees, and the board itself. This cost is largely unavoidable, if successfully implementing the 33 Principles is to be achieved.

What is the scope of the proposed reporting requirements? The 38 proposed by-laws establish some 20 reporting requirements, including annual reports, semiannual reports, quarterly reports, and periodic reports based on reportable or triggering events. The number, type, and proposed by-law creating the reporting requirements are as follows: 10 annual requirements (by-laws 1-A, 1-C, 2-A, 7-A, 7-C, 11-A, 16-A, 21-A, 24-A, and 25-A), one semiannual report (by-law 5-C), three quarterly reports (by-laws 4-C, 6-C, and 21-A), and six periodic reports (by-laws 2-A, 8-A, 11-A, 27-A, 28-A, and 30-A). The proposed by-laws create this general level of reporting burden. Boards implementing the 33 Principles must determine the size of reporting burden the organization can incur to implement the principles. Alternatively, the board may determine what other organizational activities are of lower priority than improved governance and accountability, and then reorder its priorities and resources accordingly.

In addition to the reporting requirements, for each principle a decision was made as to where compliance responsibility would lie. Providing the necessary information is the first step. Who will evaluate and act upon the information? In most cases, the responsible decision-makers are internal representatives including the president and various board committees (nominating committee, compliance committee, resource and fundraising committee, etc.) or the whole board. In some cases, the enforcement agent is an external party, such as with the by-law implementing the cooperative processes and whistleblower provision of Principle 4, by-law 4-C, Option 2, which proposes the establishment of an external ombud panel. Other examples of using external compliance agents include Principles 29, 32, and 33, and by-laws 27-B, 27-C, and 27-D. These by-law provisions require that certain organizational commitments be publicly reported to create a self-monitoring mechanism based on public feedback. Boards implementing any of the 33 Principles can use either internal or external agents, or a combination, and achieve certain efficiencies by shifting the burden of monitoring and reporting outside of the organization. Aside from administrative burdens posed by reporting requirements that enable compliance and enforcement, the board will experience significant time burdens. This latter burden may be moderated in many ways prospectively by seeking board members with related experience and expertise in such matters, increasing in-person or electronic board meetings and relying upon mediation-type processes to facilitate board decision making, to name a few.

7

Options for Boards

How is a board to proceed from here? Two hurdles to implementation include consensus and cost issues. Regarding consensus, the approach proposed here is for nonprofits to start implementing those principles on which consensus should be easy or relatively easy to achieve. If a by-law approach to implementation is relied upon, as recommended here, boards may proceed directly themselves. Hiring outside consultants is not necessary with a by-law approach. Moreover, over half of the principles appear relatively amenable to board consensus: 1, 2, 5, 9, 10, 11, 13, 14, 15, 18, 19, 21, 22, 26, 27, 29, 31, and 33. The approach recommended here is to implement any and all individual principles for which board consensus can most easily be reached and not to postpone implementation until agreement is reached on other principles, where consensus may be more challenging, elusive, or in some cases, not possible. This step will require some balancing due to the interrelationship of issues, as noted previously. This is, however, one way to make immediate, incremental progress in implementing as many principles as possible, as called for by Independent Sector (IS Panel 2007), which states, "**The key is to begin that process today**" (7, emphasis in original).

A second hurdle is cost. Many principles, however, are not resource intensive in their implementation, or are ethics related, and should pose relatively little incremental cost burden. Those principles, again over half, appear to include: 2, 3, 5, 7, 9, 10, 11, 12, 13, 14, 15, 17, 20, 22, 23, 24, 25, 26, 27, 28, 29, 30, 31, 32, and 33. With regard to startup costs, smaller organizations with limited budgets could seek modest grants from foundations with a commitment to governance, accountability, or self-regulation. Grants of less than \$5,000 should enable nonprofits to implement many, or all, of the 33 Principles. Such funding could help cover facilitation costs, meeting overhead, and some legal consultation. Another option is for Independent Sector to contact various foundations to explore their willingness to offer such grants to fund implementation of the 33 Principles on Self-Regulation. IS potentially could be the catalyst for such funding. A second advantage is that a foundation, as part of its funding and evaluation process, would understandably assess progress and implementation, as it approves and releases the funds. Another option is for Independent Sector to solicit from the legal and nonprofit management academic and consultant communities any members willing to provide pro-bono, or heavily discounted, services to aid all nonprofits willing to commit publicly to implement the 33 Principles on Self-Regulation. A fourth option would be for nonprofit organizations, perhaps geographically linked or by mission, to join together in an effort to minimize incremental startup costs, sharing meeting costs, legal expenses, and so on.[note] In the review of the 65 sets of by-laws, it appeared that some by-laws had similarities among nonprofits that shared similar missions; some level of partnership or other mutual cooperation may already exist. Many resource-attracting, or resource-sharing, options appear to exist at both the organization and sector levels of intervention, as noted above, for organizations serious about implementing the 33 Principles.

NOTE

1. As laws vary by state, consultation with counsel is needed to ensure that by-laws comply with applicable statutes; joint efforts by nonprofits could achieve synergies and reduce start-up costs significantly.

8

Conclusion

An organization can put in place a highly effective strategy for advancing self-regulation through implementing best practices within the organization's by-laws (Corbett 1995; 1996; 2007) and creating mediating structures at organizational and sector levels of intervention (Corbett 1998; 2000a). Further, as described here, some 38 by-laws were developed based, in part, on the examination of 65 sets of by-laws from A-rated nonprofits in an effort to implement IS's proposed 33 Principles on Self-Regulation. A notable strength in using by-laws is that they are a powerful, common denominator of nonprofit governance; they are common to all sizes of formal nonprofits and, therefore, provide a strategy that is virtually universal. This strategy and approach are empirically grounded and designed to be useful to, and usable by, small- and medium-sized nonprofits as well.

No doubt other strategies and methods of implementation can be developed other than a by-law approach. But what are they, and are they more likely to succeed? Will they be enforceable? Will they endure or merely constitute short-term lip service? This is a challenge for researchers and practitioners alike. What other strategies and approaches exist—or can be quickly developed—to enable all nonprofits to evolve and improve their own governance and self-regulation, consistent with the 33 Principles on Self-Regulation? The identification of additional, competing strategies would be beneficial and create additional options for nonprofits serious about improved self-regulation and implementing the 33 Principles.

Regardless of the strategy or method used, however, many of the 33 Principles appear to present fairly low consensus or cost hurdles. Therefore, based on this examination, substantial progress in self-regulation and improved governance of nonprofit organizations appears realistically achievable—and ultimately may prove more a function of organizational will and fortitude than overcoming substantive resource or consensus constraints. As a result, nonprofits with the will and fortitude to improve their governance and accountability by implementing the 33 Principles should be able to move forward, immediately, with any and all principles upon which consensus can be built. Nor are boards prevented from adopting stricter standards where they desire, such as identified in many of the proposed 38 by-laws, with the various options.

Industry feedback should prove useful for boards to consider as they move forward at this critical juncture for improved governance and self-regulation. For example, in response to the proposed principles, Berns (2007) offers several constructive simple steps to strengthen and expand the system of self-regulation (76). Those steps include greater reliance on accreditation systems and peer review, calls to action from IS and other nonprofit leaders, increased pressure on grant makers to fund self-regulation for small and medium-sized organizations, and greater recognition by funders for nonprofits that have obtained third-party accreditation. Berns also recommends that nonprofits that have obtained such accreditation promote it with donors so they will know that such reviews matter (76). He also notes that it must be clear that self-regulation cannot be achieved if charities do little more than read, consider, and endorse a set of principles (76). Clearly, Berns's comments convey a deep sense of concern about the future of the sector and appear to be an urgent call to action for sector leaders and organizations, now that the Principles on Self-Regulation have been issued.

Trent Stamp of *Charity Navigator* has voiced additional concerns. He fears that many nonprofits that we think are reputable will only give lip service to the standards but won't follow them in the long run (Michaels 2007, 65). By-law implementation, however, should mitigate such concerns as well-structured, board-approved by-laws—with aggressive reporting requirements and improved public transparency—could significantly document compliance.

The time is ripe for nonprofits, large and small, to determine what actions, if any, they will take to adopt these principles—and how, if at all, they will put them into practice. To its credit, Independent Sector has embarked on a highly complex, and apparently unprecedented, task of consensus building and public participation involving many hundreds of participants and representatives from within and outside the sector. Since IS began this effort in October 2004, at the request of the Senate Finance Committee, over 90 private foundations, community foundations, corporate giving programs, and nonprofits contributed $3.5 million to support the work of the committee, which included some 24 foundation and charity leaders (Michaels 2007, 65).

While many have expended great resources and effort and the 33 Principles have been issued, this fight is not over. Clearly, the future of the sector lies in the hands of many sector leaders, funders, and nonprofit organizations of all sizes that will determine whether and to what extent significant, documentable strides in preventive, proactive, self-regulation of the sector will actually occur. Or, alternatively, if the loud call from our elected and industry leaders for improved self-regulation goes unheeded— in the next round with the regulator, the sector will very likely be absorbing some very heavy blows from new, burdensome, government-imposed regulation from the state level, the federal level—or more likely, from both.

References

Note: Every effort has been made to ensure that the URLs are accurate and up to date. However, with the rapid changes that occur on the World Wide Web, it is inevitable that some pages or other resources will have been discontinued or moved, and some content modified or reorganized. The publisher recommends that readers who cannot locate sources or information they seek with the URLs cited use one of the many search engines available on the Internet.

ADR Pledge. 2007. *The pledge.* International Institute for Conflict Prevention and Resolution. www.cpradr.org (accessed October 25, 2007).
———. 2010. *About the Pledge.* International Institute for Conflict Prevention and Resolution. www.cpradr.org.

American Bar Association. 2007. *Guide to resolving legal disputes: Inside and outside the courtroom.* New York: Random House.

American Institute of Philanthropy (AIP). 1995. *Charity rating guide and watchdog report.* November/December. 1–16.

BBB Wise Giving Guide. 2009. *Standards for charity accountability: Wise giving guide.* Arlington, VA: Better Business Bureau Wise Giving Alliance. Spring.

Berns, Peter V. 2007. A missed opportunity to ensure real charity accountability. *Chronicle of Philanthropy* (November 1): 76.

BoardSource and Independent Sector. 2006. *The Sarbanes-Oxley Act and implications for nonprofit organizations.* www.independentsector.org/sarbanes_oxley.

Chait, Richard P., Thomas P. Holland, and Barbara B. Taylor. 1996. *Improving the performance of governing boards.* Westport, CT: Oryx Press.

Christensen, Rachel A., and Alnoor Ebrahim. 2006. How does accountability affect mission? *Nonprofit Management and Leadership* 17, no. 2: 195–209.

Corbett, Christopher. 1995. *Exploring nonprofit dysfunction: A rationale, expectations, and a proposed model.* Paper presented at the Annual Conference of the Association for Research on Nonprofit Organizations and Voluntary Action, Cleveland, November 2–4.

————. 1996. *Preventing and remediating nonprofit dysfunction: Enabling trustee participation for more effective governance.* Paper presented at the Annual Conference of Association for Research on Nonprofit Organizations and Voluntary Action, New York, November 7–9.

————. 1998. *A nonprofit in crisis: Implications for governance and regulatory solutions. An HMO case study.* Paper presented at the Annual Conference of the Association for Research on Nonprofit Organizations and Voluntary Action, Seattle, November 5–7.

————. 2000a. *Regulation in the public interest: More government or improved self-regulation?* Poster presented at the Annual Conference of the Association for Research on Nonprofit Organizations and Voluntary Action, New Orleans, November 16–18.

————. 2000b. Commentary. *Nonprofit Management and Leadership* 10, no. 3: 341–44.

————. 2001. *Testimony presented before New York State Legislature, Assembly Task Force on People with Disabilities* at hearing on New York State's Compliance with the Americans with Disabilities Act, March 27, 2001. Prefiled direct testimony (1–7) with cross-examination (241–53). Albany: New York State Legislature.

————. 2005. Stewardship of public assets under nonprofit conversion models: NY's Blue Cross Blue Shield case study. *Nonprofit Management and Leadership* 16, no. 2: 153–69.

————. 2007. *Preventing and remediating board bias in nonprofit organizations.* Poster presented at the Annual Conference of the Association for Research on Nonprofit Organizations and Voluntary Action, Atlanta, November 15–17.

CPR Annual Report. 2006. *Annual report of the International Institute for Conflict Prevention and Resolution.* www.cpradr.org (accessed October 25, 2007).

Dalton, James H., Maurice J. Elias, and Abraham Wandersman. 2001. *Community psychology: Linking individuals and communities.* Belmont, CA: Wadsworth.

Galaskiewicz, Joseph. 2003. The president's message. *ARNOVA News* 32, no. 2: 3.

Grassley, Charles E., and Max Baucus. 2004. Letter dated September 22, 2004, to Diana Aviv, president, Independent Sector. www.nonprofitpanel.org/report/final/. 110–11.

Heller, Kenneth, Richard Price, Shulamit Reinharz, Stephanie Riger, and Abraham Wandersman. 1984. *Psychology and Community Change.* Homewood, IL: Dorsey.

Henry, James F., and Jethro K. Lieberman. 1985. *The manager's guide to resolving legal disputes: Better results without litigation.* New York: Harper & Row.

IS Accountability. 2004. *Statement of values and code of ethics for nonprofit and philanthropic organizations.* Model code for all 501(c)(3) and 501(c)(4) organizations. February 3. 1–5. www.independentsector.org (accessed September 17, 2007).

IS Panel. 2007. *Principles for good governance and ethical practice: A guide for charities and foundations.* Reference edition. Panel on nonprofit sector convened by Independent Sector. www.independentsector.org.

Jackson, Peggy M., and Toni E. Fogarty. 2005. *Sarbanes-Oxley for nonprofits: A guide to building competitive advantage.* Hoboken, NJ: Wiley & Sons.

———. 2006. *Sarbanes-Oxley and nonprofit management.* Hoboken, NJ: Wiley & Sons.

Jacobs, Jerald A. 1986. *Association law handbook.* Washington, DC: Bureau of National Affairs.

Lindblom, Charles E. 1990. *Inquiry and change: The troubled attempt to understand and shape society.* New Haven, CT: Yale University Press.

———, and David K. Cohen. 1979. *Usable knowledge: Social science and social problem solving.* New Haven, CT: Yale University Press.

Michaels, Marty. 2007. Committee of nonprofit leaders issues set of accountability guidelines. *Chronicle of Philanthropy* (November 1): 65.

Oleck, Howard L., and Martha E. Stewart. 1994. *Nonprofit corporations, organizations and associations.* Englewood Cliffs, NJ: Prentice Hall.

Panel on the Nonprofit Sector. 2007a. *List of those who have signed on to the panel's final report.* www.nonprofitpanel.org/Report/final/signers.html.

———. 2007b. *Panel on the nonprofit sector draft principles for effective practice—second comment period, comments due March 30, 2007.* www.nonprofitpanel.org/selfreg/ (accessed September 17, 2007).

———. 2007c. *Panel on the nonprofit sector invites comment on principles on self-regulation.* Press release dated January 12, 2007. www.nonprofitpanel.org/press/PR_Panel_Invites_Comments_SelfReg_html/index.html.

Young, Dennis R., Neil Bania, and Darlyne Bailey. 1996. Structure and accountability: A study of national nonprofit associations. *Nonprofit Management and Leadership* 6, no. 4: 347–65.

Index

Jasper, James M., xi
Jonestown massacre, xii

The Klan (Sims), xi

Lavigne, Yves, xi
Lee, Martha F., xi
Levitas, Daniel, xi
Lewis, J. R., xi
The Lifestyle: A Look at the Erotic Rites of Swingers (Gould), xi
litigation, ADR Pledge and, 15–17
Longwood, W. Merle, xii

media
  as electronic, 30, 39, 54, 76
  nonprofit coverage by, ix
Melton, J. Gordon, xi
mission, of nonprofit, 3, 46–47, 54, 56–57, 67

NC. *See* Nominating Committee
Nelkin, Dorothy, xi
NGOs. *See* nonprofits and foundations
Nominating Committee (NC), 35–37, 41–43
nomination, to board, 5, 10, 33–37, 41–43
non-governmental organizations (NGOs). *See* nonprofits and foundations
Nonprofit and Voluntary Sector Quarterly (*NVSQ*) (journal), xvii
The Nonprofit Quarterly (journal), xiii
nonprofits and foundations. *See also* board, nonprofit; by-laws, nonprofit
  accountability by, ix, xi, xiii, 2–3, 46–47, 54, 56–57, 67, 75
  accreditation for, 3, 80

ADR for, 14, 15–18
articles of incorporation for, 45–46
assets of, 22–23
audit of, 51–52, 54–55
BBB and, 57
benchmarks for, 56–57
budget for, 29–30, 38, 52–54, 56–57, 77–78
CEO for, 9–10, 23–25, 30, 38–39, 41, 54–56, 68–69
compensation by, 38–39, 48–49, 54–56, 69
competition between, ix–x
compliance by, ix, xi, xiii–xvii, xxi–xxii, 1–5, 6nn2–3, 9–10, 24–25, 46, 76–77, 78n1, 79–81
conflict of interest within, 11–13, 16, 18, 39–40, 45–46, 48, 55–56, 66–67
cooperative processes for, 14–18, 76, 78
CPR Institute services for, 16, 18
dissolution of, 23, 24, 63–64
donations to, x, xii, 61–67, 70–72, 80
ethics code for, 1, 9–14, 39–41, 45–46, 48, 55–56, 66–69
evaluation of, xii, 26–27, 30, 33, 38–39, 42–45
Expense Reimbursement Policy for, 58–60
expenses of, 2, 5–6, 13, 47, 75, 77
fundraising by, x, 56–57, 61–62, 64–65, 69–72
government contracts and funding for, x
government oversight of, x, xiii–xiv, xxi, 1, 14, 18–20, 42, 46
grants for, 77–78
immunity of, xii
insurance for, 23–25

Also from Kumarian Press...

Civil Society and NGOs:

From Political Won't to Political Will:
Building Support for Participatory Governance
Edited by Carmen Malena

For the Love of God:
NGOs and Religious Identity in a Violent World
Shawn Flanigan

The Change Imperative: Creating the Next-Generation NGO
Paul Ronalds

NGOs in International Politics
Shamima Ahmed and David Potter

New and Forthcoming:

Philanthropy and the Nonprofit Sector: An Introduction
Ken Menkhaus

Creative Capacity Development:
Learning to Adapt in Development Practice
Jenny Pearson

The Politics of Collective Advocacy in India: Tools and Traps
Nandini Deo and Duncan McDuie-Ra

Evading Disparities:
The Limits of Social Capital in Rural Development
Antonio de la Peña

Visit Kumarian Press at www.kpbooks.com or call **toll-free**
800.232.0223 for a complete catalog.

DATE DUE	RETURNED

Kumarian Press, located in Sterling, Virginia, is a forward-looking, scholarly press that promotes active international engagement and an awareness of global connectedness.